Crystal Clear
Communication

Crystal Clear Communication

How to Communicate Anything Clearly in Speech and Writing

Dr. Gary S. Goodman

MEDIA

Published 2019 by Gildan Media LLC
aka G&D Media
www.GandDmedia.com

Front Cover design by David Rheinhardt of Pyrographx

Interior design by Meghan Day Healey of Story Horse, LLC

Library of Congress Cataloging-in-Publication Data is available upon request

ISBN: 978-1-7225-0192-1

10 9 8 7 6 5 4 3 2 1

Contents

Introduction and Overview
1

Chapter 1

Begin with a Crystal clear Mind
5

Chapter 2

The Art of Preparing Crystal clear Messages
29

Chapter 3

Secrets of Appealing to Any Listener or Reader
43

Chapter 4

Special Communication Challenges and Circumstances
81

Chapter 5

Staying Positive
95

Chapter 6

Script Your Success
117

Introduction and Overview

I'm an optimist. I believe we can communicate clearly with nearly anyone.

Yes, it takes sustained effort, strategies, and techniques, and we have to overcome false starts, numerous distractions, and obstacles.

Occasionally, we have to face down prejudice, hostility, ignorance, and long odds. Our lives and careers might even be on the line.

But if we're clear about what we wish to get across, and we learn enough about our audiences and then craft and deliver an excellent, comprehensible, and appealing message, we're likely to succeed.

Let me tell you a story about someone who did just this.

In the early 1970s, with the Vietnam War still raging, Jim determined he was a conscientious objector.

"War is wrong!" he told himself, his family, and anyone that would listen.

Above all, he told this to his draft board, which had the solemn task of determining whether would-be hold-outs such as Jim would be permitted to stay out of battle, serving instead in the medical corps or in civilian capacities identified as being in the nation's interest.

There were several tests for conscientious objection, which survive to this day. An applicant for this status needs to demonstrate:

1. He is against *all* wars. He can't pick and choose the ones he agrees and disagrees with.
2. The objection needs to arise out of deeply felt religious or personal beliefs.

Although it's not widely known, there is another criterion:

3. The candidate must demonstrate his sincerity not only in written documentation and in testimony before his draft board. Optimally, he should make a *public declaration* that he is opposed to war.

Knowledgeable people told Jim the odds against being granted conscientious-objector (CO) status were about 20 to 1. Typically, if you were denied, these were the options:

1. Enlist to avoid assignment to a war zone, violating your principles.
2. Refuse induction and go to federal prison for several years.
3. Flee to Canada or to another country that would grant asylum, renouncing your American citizenship.

Jim had faith he wouldn't have to resort to any of these dodges.

One day, he saw the now-infamous news photo of actress Jane Fonda posing in front of North Vietnamese artillery while wearing a military helmet.

His jaw dropped.

He wrote a letter to a major newspaper decrying her partisanship. His crystal clear message was simple and from the heart:

"She says she's antiwar, but that means she can't take sides. As a conscientious objector, I know the difference. If you're antiwar, you're against all wars, period."

When he arrived at his draft board for his "sincerity" hearing several weeks later, the chairman said to his colleagues: "I don't know if all of you have seen Jim's letter to the editor about Jane Fonda, but you should. I think it speaks clearly and persuasively about his sincerity as a conscientious objector."

Jim was granted his CO status, and he served the country in a noncombatant role, earning an honorable discharge from the Army after eighteen months of duty.

When your life, your freedom, and your sincerity are on the line, you need a breakthrough in communication. You may have only one shot at getting your point across.

We also need to strive for crystal clear communications every day to address common challenges and opportunities in our personal lives and on the job. This is what this book aims to teach you to achieve.

Chapter One

Begin with a Crystal clear Mind

It's one thing to urge you to create crystal clear communications, but what if you simply aren't ready to get down to business?

It's very possible you haven't quieted your mind to be in the proper mood to write or to speak effectively.

Possibly you haven't truly clarified your intentions. What is my point? Do I have one main idea I want to express, or many? Which one(s) are critical?

Am I in the proper frame of mind to communicate, or am I preoccupied with something else? Am I bristling with defensiveness when I should be level-headed and dispassionate? Have I sufficiently thought through what I hope to convey clearly?

Maybe you're waiting too long—procrastinating.

A number of practical or psychological factors might also be blocking your path to achievement. If so, you can't be expected to roar down the highway of ideas without clearing the way.

If you're like most folks, you might be burdened by fears and anxieties. Often called *writer's block* and *stage fright*, these and other widespread forms of communication apprehension might be keeping you from comfortably and clearly speaking out or composing your thoughts in writing.

According to Stanford research, fully 80 percent of Americans are shy in some circumstances. Shyness could be retarding your development. According to a much-quoted bestseller, *The Book of Lists*, speaking in public is a fear that most people rank above the fear of death!

So before we get into the do's and don'ts of crafting your message, shaping it for specific readers and listeners, making it solid, we need to make *you* solid, stripping away the concerns that even very gifted communicators have about how they come across.

Conquering State Fright

First, let's tackle stage fright. Stage fright, the fear of speaking in public or communicating verbally in someone else's immediate presence, afflicts millions of people.

Where does this fear come from? And what can we do about it?

There are several possible sources of speech apprehension. We'll explore three of them:

1. We may have no significant experience speaking to groups.

2. We imagine the worst possible outcomes: fainting dead away at a podium, moving our lips and having nothing come out, hearing our voices crack, speaking gibberish, and having people laugh not at our jokes but at us.

3. Ego is a problem at both extremes of the continuum. If we lack a strong one, suffering from low self-esteem, we'll believe we haven't earned the right to speak, feeling that we're impostors. And if we think we're top guns in the speaking world, there is always a fear lurking that this time, when we reach the sound barrier, we won't soar to war speed but crash and burn.

Let's look at these problems and see what we can do to cure them.

First, what can you do if you don't have much public speaking experience? That's easy. Get more now! You can take public-speaking classes and volunteer for opportunities that force you to deliver reports and interact before groups.

How can we avoid imagining awful outcomes? That's pretty easy too. With more experience, you'll find out that few of the horrible things that you have paraded across the screen of your imagination ever occur.

Your voice *will* work, perhaps somewhat quietly at first; still, it will perform as designed.

You won't faint away, hyperventilating with chest pains. If you remember to *breathe in advance*, you will avoid *oxygen debt*—that shallowness of breath that has you racing desperately to catch yours.

If you can remember to smile at your group, they will generally return the favor. That will relax you, and if you flub up a bit, they'll give you supportive feedback.

Plus—and this is key, so please do yourself the favor of remembering it—YOU WILL NEVER APPEAR AS NERVOUS TO OTHERS AS YOU DO TO YOURSELF. Only you can hear that heart thumping in your chest, and only you feel the clamminess of your hands. Now that you do, forget about them.

Which leads me to the point about ego. Typically, when we're experiencing a fear of failure, we are fixated on the wrong thing: ourselves. When you're about to speak, try to adopt a "We do it all for you" attitude (to borrow from a fast-food chain's slogan). When you focus on your message, you deemphasize yourself, and your audience will respond accordingly.

But one of my ultimate tips is to RELAX UNTIL IT IS TOO LATE!

Keynote speakers, top salespeople, and big-time athletes face a similar challenge.

How do you get up for the game and get ready to do your best without nervously dissipating your energy or overvaluing the idea of winning at any cost? In other words, how can you stay loose? How can you keep the fun in the experience instead of turning it into a gut-wrenching drag?

Something that that works for me is to monitor my nerves. When they get too jittery, this cues me to take the next step, which is to *remind myself to get nervous later, not now.*

I don't put myself down for getting the butterflies, which is an easy trap to fall into for a professional keynote speaker and sales coach. In effect, I say to myself, "Of course you want to feel nervous, and you'll get your chance later, closer to kickoff time."

Then something marvelous happens. I really relax. I enjoy myself. I enhance my upcoming event with some new twists. I might even decide to add a new celebrity impression (say, Sean Connery) to my "act." Of course, while all of this relaxing and fun prep are going on, the clock is ticking away, and I'm not sweating it.

Then it's thirty seconds until I'm on, and guess what? It's too late to worry!

This has worked for me so many times, in so many settings, that I feel it is nearly foolproof.

Try it for yourself, and please tell me how you do!

Appreciate this: *even professionals sweat a little!*

Ask experienced actors and speakers if they are at least a little nervous before an event, and typically they'll reply: "Of course; that never completely goes away!" Many will add these crucial words: "And if I don't have at least a few butterflies in my stomach, then something is wrong, and I run the risk of giving a flat performance."

One more thing: *use an audience grabber to start your talk.*

"One in two people between the ages of fifty-five and seventy-five will need long-term care in a nursing facility or at home, with the assistance of a nurse or other health-services provider.

"Some will break their hips and others may develop Alzheimer's, but still, the statistic is one in two.

"How many of you have a long-term care health plan in place that enables you to choose to be treated in your own home or in a facility of your choice?

"How many of you can afford the hundreds of dollars a day, $6000 per month and more, year after year without selling most if not all of your assets or becoming a burden to your families?"

Before you get swept up in responding to these devices, let me say that I've just exposed you to two great ways of opening a speech: (1) the startling statistic and (2) the direct question.

Here I've blended them, but you could use either one to grab your audience's attention. And that word definitely applies to the use of a special technique to begin your talk: you want to develop a *grabber*. Ideally, this will snap people out of the doldrums and focus their attention right away. Moreover, especially if you're in a commercial setting and your purpose is to sell, these tools help you to establish a need and its significance right off the bat.

Most well-prepared speakers will have statistics and questions somewhere in their talks, but somewhere isn't good enough. They need to be strategically placed.

For example, the other evening I was assessing the skills of a group of financial-services marketers that use the platform to sell senior citizens—you guessed it—long-term health care. But instead of placing the devices in the right place, they erred by burying them in the body of the talk.

That statistic—that one in two will need this care—is attention-getting. Why wait until you're a half-hour into the chat to mention it?

Journalists call this habit of inserting the juiciest morsel too late *burying the lead*, and watchful editors catch this flaw over and again.

By making sure that you have a strategic grabber, you'll avoid this mistake, make the most of your research and your subject, and be much more persuasive and successful with audiences.

Plus, when you see your audience is with you from the start, responding to your content with keen interest, your stage fright will quickly evaporate, to be replaced by calm and steady self-assurance.

Writer's Block: The Sword of Disapproval

As a toddler, I'd scribble with very serious intent and then whisk my document to my mom for her appraisal.

"Ah," she'd say. "Very nice."

I'd return reinforced and emboldened to my ultra-important ministrations.

At some point my older brother and sister would amble along, grab the sheet from my hand, and wise-crack, "Someday this will mean something!"

And their point was. . . ?

I'm still trying to impress with my writing. (It helps to know the alphabet.) But if I become overly concerned with how people are responding to my work, I cut back on my production, which is probably what my siblings had in mind.

If we let that happen, we're succumbing to writer's block. Unabated, that impulse to please can completely squeeze off our creative spigots.

Wanting to spread happiness and cheer seems quite natural, and to this day, when I am complimented on my books and articles, my heart soars. But seeking a reward of this kind leads to doom.

When we give people the power to praise, we also give them the sword of disapproval to wield above our heads. When someone becomes a reward source, they also become a potential punisher.

A bad word, or a kind one withheld, can send us careening down a Grand Canyon of self-doubt. While we're decoding what they are telling us, ferreting out truths in their text and tone, we're running from the next page that needs to be written.

Pleasing and writing simultaneously is impossible. Choose one or the other. But be warned: if you choose to please, you're also very possibly choosing a writer's block.

Did Your Teachers Contribute to Your Writer's Block?

I suspect there are two kinds of writers: (1) those that were schooled by language teachers and (2) those that were schooled despite language teachers.

I'm a teacher, so I would not minimize the importance of teachers. They are so crucial to our development that having bad ones is a special curse. Fortunately, many recover.

For instance, I know a foreign-born American whose English teacher in her native country predicted: "You'll never learn this language!"

Nice comment, right?

The student became fluent in English, thank you very much! She learned despite the negative influence of her teacher.

Many of us learn to write professionally in the same way. We've received standard or substandard instruction, but our desire to excel strips away the barnacles of self-doubt that were attached to our skimpy skiffs when we first set sail. Leaving the brutish harbor of academia, we venture out to a placid sea of relatively grand achievement.

My first journalism professor flunked me in publicity and gave me a meager C in feature writing. I went on to become a best-selling author of thirty books, more than 1500 articles, and other items too many to recount here,

And my instructor—what became of her? Nothing notable, but I suspect she came across my name here and there or heard me on radio or watched me on TV.

If you suffer from writer's block, it may be traceable to your early influences, and especially to incapable or mean-spirited instructors. I suggest you perform a mental feat called *recapitulation*. Anthropologist Carlos Castaneda describes this in his books as mentally reviewing all of the people you've known, breathing in what you recall of what was said between you, and then dispatching those memories to oblivion with an out breath. According to Castaneda, this practice will dissipate the negative charge that they injected into your life.

Start with your language and communications teachers. You just might discover one of the most profound sources of your writer's block, which you'll then be able to deep-six.

Why Do Writers Block Themselves?

Blaming others only gets us so far. We are the ones in charge of our development, at least at this point. So we need to take responsibility for our challenges and then constructively act on them.

As writers, we tend to block ourselves for five reasons:
1. We have nothing to say.
2. We're timid about saying what we want to say.
3. We feel we've said it before, and said it better.
4. We've been shamed by someone who has less talent, yet the criticism is sticking to us like egg on a car's fake chrome.
5. We're afraid to see how bad our writing really is.

Let's take these in order.
1. I like Robert Pirsig's advice in his book *Zen and the Art of Motorcycle Maintenance*. The protagonist's rhetoric students couldn't seem to get started on an essay about Bozeman, Montana. So he nudged them by saying, "Write about one street." They balked, so he

went on to suggest writing about one building. That still didn't work. OK, he advised, write about *one brick* in one building in Bozeman, Montana.

Having nothing to say isn't a problem. Get passionate about that fact. Hate it. Seethe with disdain, and then vent your spleen.

I was so upset by the village idiots I encountered as a coach in my daughter's sports leagues that I wrote a book about it. Gosh, it felt great to get some payback for the idiocy I withstood.

2. Being timid is really about being secretly grandiose. Your problem is, you don't know what you'll do with all the attention you're going to get from your wonderful writing. That's fear of success. Forget about it until you're inundated with paid offers and by an adoring press.

3. *Everything* has been said before, and most of us cannot avoid being somewhat derivative. There is a good chance that you'll say it differently, and better this time.

4. The people who shame you are not comfy in their own skin. They're abusers, having themselves been abused. Plus, they're jealous. And you're taking their opinions seriously?

5. Poor writing is a precursor to great writing. You can always revise, but getting something on the page NOW is your marching order.

Go to it!

When we conjure up the image of someone plagued by writer's block, usually a literary person comes to mind, someone who is otherwise adept at putting paws to the keyboard or ink to a page.

But businesspeople may suffer the most from writer's block. My experience in business, as a sales manager, management consultant, entrepreneur, and publisher, tells me that this stereotype only reveals part of the story.

Most sufferers of writer's block don't know they're blocked. This is partly because they don't define themselves as writers. Their occupational titles would include nearly everyone in business who didn't go to college or who barely scraped by with passing grades in communication courses if they did. Blocks blight even the best and brightest MBAs and attorneys.

"I hate writing emails," some lament.

"Performance appraisals drive me nuts!" managers complain.

"I spend way too much time writing my speeches," senior executives observe.

What they don't say—which they would if they wrote more or if they were professional scribes—is, "I'm blocked!"

Once that fact becomes known and appreciated, remedial measures can be taken.

What would the same blocked executives do to overcome a sales slump? If their sales flagged, they'd endeavor to put more prospects into their pipelines, thus improving the odds that they would develop enough yesses to keep them afloat. In a phrase, they'd work the law of large numbers, seeking out every chance to improve their writing by eagerly doing as much of it as possible.

But without a diagnosis of writer's block, they're likely to avoid writing situations, which only exacerbates the problem.

Let's reach out to businesspeople to assist them with this problem. Maybe they can reciprocate by showing writers how to earn a buck!

Beat Writer's Block Today!

So far I've implied that writer's block is a malady that occurs more by choice than by chance, and there are even perverse satisfactions we glean from it, including sympathy and attention from others. Here are five things you can do to beat it today:

1. Write your name on the blackboard 100 times. Remember that schoolroom punishment? I'm half-joking here. What you need to do is write ANYTHING, of whatever quality, and even of the briefest length, and simply file it away. Congratulations! You will have produced SOMETHING, and that beats nothing.

2. Read one of the hundreds of thousands of articles at EzineArticles.com or a similar site. Compare the quality you see with the quality of your work. Believe me, you'll find some stinkers, but they're out there, aren't they?

3. Realize there are no great articles or books or emails: just FINISHED ones and the other kind. During

my PhD program, some of my fiends who had already completed their degrees consoled me with these words.

4. Commit to writing at least one page every day, if only by keeping a daily journal in which you rant. Nobody should see this notebook but you. Before long, you'll write more effortlessly, and then the quality will kick in. Then, by writing a page a day of real stuff, you'll have a finished book manuscript in a year, or less.

5. Don't critique your own work, and pay no heed to the gratuitous critiques of others. About 700 articles ago, I stopped paying attention to the comments people file in response to my online articles. Frankly, Scarlett, I don't give a hoot what they think, and neither should you. Taking criticism personally or too seriously will only slow you down. Don't let that happen!

Finally, beat writer's block by *getting something, ANYTHING, onto the page*!

Ray Bradbury said a real writer can write anything, and I'm starting to believe him. Your task could be crafting a technical manual, shaping a haiku, composing a theme for an advertising campaign, or (as those of us in business do) developing conversation plans and call paths to promote purchases and retain clients. If you are a writer, you can do it all, though you might have a special gift with a particular subset of scribing.

No matter what your forte might be, the essential thing every real writer knows is that you absolutely must BEGIN somewhere.

Among other things, I write scripts for sales and customer-service conversations. Though I am called on to draft unique presentations each time, I always begin with a pat phrase or question. In outbound calling it might be, "Hello, Mr./Ms. Blank?"

At that moment some wonderful things happen. For one thing, the next phrase or sentence comes out by itself. Generally, it doesn't need much coaxing, and if it is running late, all I do is reread the opener that I've already put down on the page. It may not be flawless, but it transports me to the following passage, and so forth. Before I know it, I have a draft of the basic conversation.

The genesis of this working document is, again, that standard starter. Mine makes sense; it's pertinent to what follows. But for the purpose of beating writer's block, and becoming productive, yours could be gibberish yet still have value.

The key: get something, ANYTHING, onto the page!

Are You Ready?

It's about five in the morning, and I've already been awake for a half an hour. I lumber out of bed and descend the stairs to my home office and see that it's only one o'clock, and yet I'm in no mood to fight for more sleep.

What woke me up is an email that I received from a colleague that I'm recruiting for a business conference. He asked me about five questions—all of them pertinent to the occasion and to his potential role as a presenter.

I feel uncomfortable about responding. Yet I know it would be rude and inefficient to not get back to him in a timely way.

I'm in a bind. I need to write promptly, yet I feel something is preventing me from writing. I'm feeling blocked, but why?

I'll analyze this for you in a moment, but first let me make this point: to communicate clearly, we have to be ready and remove any obstacles.

Which ones are preventing me from doing my duty? For one thing, I didn't have answers to all of his questions, appropriate as they were. And this made me feel insecure.

Let's examine these problems and their potential solutions.

1. Why do I have to have suitable answers at that very moment? The occasion is more than a month away— plenty of time to discover and to convey the missing details.

2. Did not having *all* of the information really preclude me from sharing *some* of it with my contact? Of course not! Where is it written that I must cover everything in a single message?

3. What the heck is wrong with being up front, with saying outright, "I don't yet have all of the details"? Is this a crime?

4. What if I only cover the points he raised that I am comfortable with and simply skip the rest for now? If the ones I pass on are important, he'll raise them again, or I'll take some time to discover the answers and volunteer them in short order.

5. Did all of his questions *deserve* to be answered, and if so, now? There are folks that will listen to a speech you'll make, and they specialize in asking irrelevant and even embarrassing questions. Politicians face this all the time from adversaries and from the press. Real pros simply answer the question in a way that highlights what they want to say, or they duck it with humor or redesign it: "What I think you're really asking is X."

But there was something even deeper going on here, another set of agendas that prevented me from comfortably responding to my associate's email right away.

I was concerned that if I gave him too many details about the event, he would find a way to steal the engagement from me. This, or its equivalent, has happened to me twice that I know of in my career. So from a self-protective standpoint, I didn't want to overexplain so that he could reverse-engineer the deal and try to take it over.

Another feature of this scenario was the fact that my client, who was putting on the event, asked me to bring in or recommend some colleagues that could join me in speaking. He was pressing me for some names, but I had yet to receive his deposit on my fee.

Dun & Bradstreet used to have an expression that comes to mind: THE DEAL ISN'T MADE UNTIL THE MONEY IS PAID.

I hope you'll commit that crystal clear comment to memory and refer to it often.

So I'm the go-between who, if he isn't careful, could become the odd man out. Which would argue quite convincingly for slowing the movie down. As you know, in football and basketball, teams have a certain number of time-outs that they can draw upon. They use them to slow down the pace of the game, especially if opponents seem to be scoring like crazy or their own team is making a spate of mistakes.

Likewise, in a negotiation, which of course is a communication, sometimes it pays to drag your feet a little. Your counterpart might be going at warp speed, but this doesn't mean you need to put the pedal to the metal as well.

Let's take a moment to summarize where I am in this situation: (1) I'm being pressed by two individuals for information, (2) some of which I had, and (3) if I offered too much information too soon, it could backfire and I could lose my end of the deal.

Was there another option?

Could I simply spell out my concerns to both of them? Would it be viable to say, "I'll be in a better position to steer you to an additional speaker or to give you additional details when I have received my deposit for this event?" That's crystal clear, isn't it? Is there a major down side to saying it explicitly?

I can think of two right off the bat:

1. It might say, "I don't trust you," which is insulting, even if true. For instance, I recall telling a magazine publisher that he had infringed one of my trademarks by using a phrase I registered to promote his semi-

nars. His reply, "Please send me proof. I believe in that adage, 'Trust, but verify.'" I did, but I declined to do any additional business with him because he implied that I would lie.

2. It might say, "I'm paranoid" and "I doubt my own value so much that I think a competitor can steal my clients and my clients will gladly be stolen."

Was there a middle way, a path I could take that would optimize my interests, assist my client, and inform my colleague sufficiently?

Here's what I did.

By three in the morning, I had written the email to my colleague. I told him about the three themes of the meeting, and I gave him an idea of two topics he could prepare that could be valuable to the client. I also told him what my focus would be, implying that he should steer clear of this turf. I mentioned I wasn't sure how much of his time would be required, but he should quote a fee to me for one to three days of service. This had the advantage of getting me off the hook about reciting what I was being paid.

I promptly emailed an invoice for the speaking-fee deposit to the client, requesting a check via overnight mail. While, realistically, I didn't expect such a prompt turnaround, it set the stage for expecting a check in about four business days or less. I figured within that time I could stall on delivering more information to the client and to my colleague.

Here are four learning points from this example:

1. To write clearly, you need to be ready.
2. You're not ready until you are clear about why you are reluctant to communicate.
3. Once you have identified your motivations and those of your recipients, you can get under way, but not before.
4. Playing the clock, as coaches do in sports, may be necessary for achieving the proper timing for your communications.

We Are One and the Same!

To an extent, I have avoided writing this part of the book, mainly because it might come across as overly metaphysical. But please bear with me, and I assure you it will become quite concrete. And the payoff you'll get will be substantial in promoting crystal clear communications.

My point, which I'm just going to lay out in front of you, is this:

WE SUFFER FROM AN ILLUSION OF SEPARATENESS.

I'm not the first to notice this fact about human beings. Buddhists and others have noted this for thousands of years. We look at ourselves in the mirror and conclude that we're unique. Our fingerprints tell the same story. But our true and meaningful differences are trivial. Fundamentally, we are more than simply the same. We are ONE, or, if you will, ONE AND THE SAME.

This mortal coil, the body we dwell in, certainly seems separate from everyone else's. There are objects and beings that seem completely unrelated to us—detached, off by themselves. I am not the shelf on which this finished book will one day sit. True? I don't want to bump arms with yours as I hunker down into an airplane seat; nor do you want to rub elbows with me, lest we rub each other the wrong way. I'm ME and you're YOU, and the twain shall never meet, we hope, unless it is by mutual consent, right?

Wrong.

We are one and the same. At least this is a thesis I'd like you to entertain as you prepare to speak or write. Our goals, interests, and even destinies are one and the same.

If you begin with this postulate, several interesting and positive things will happen to your speaking and writing:

1. You'll tend to make your point fast.
2. You won't waste energy in circumlocution, talking around things because you believe that you'll gain an unfair advantage in doing so.
3. You'll open up, becoming transparent to the other person.
4. And they in turn will become open and clear to you.

Let's start with point 3, shall we?

If you think you're a separate being, you'll probably avoid self-disclosure and openly discussing your aims and motivations. You'll remain cloistered, perhaps thinking that exposing your true self will be somehow offensive or alienating.

But psychologists tell us that *self-disclosure creates trust*. By becoming transparent, or crystal clear and see-through to others, they are able to overcome their illusions of separateness. They learn enough about us to determine that we are not a threat, that we are more or less seeking exactly what they seek. They identify with us, perceiving us to be substantially similar. What theorist Kenneth Burke calls *consubstantiality*, this feeling that we're made of the same stuff, is a by-product of effective communication, as well as a cause of it. But generally we don't produce this perception in others unless we start with it as our own belief.

Opening up, becoming clear and transparent, is therapeutic. We do this quite often with friends and family, and they with us. Having a great talk with a pal, where we get something off our chest or even rant and rave, is cathartic. It releases a lot of negative energy, and we come to learn that our buddies often have the same thoughts and feelings, which is reassuring.

To a lesser extent, doing the same thing, even in business and professional contexts, feels good, and delivers to us a personal payoff, as well as a favorable communication result.

I mentioned that when we open up, others are likely to reciprocate. This creates a virtuous cycle of intimacy that leads to creating better understanding and ushers efficiency and clarity into our communications.

The reverse is also true. By seeming strategic and secretive, we induce our counterparts to act the same way. Withholding vital information about ourselves creates ambiguity and uncertainty, and it feeds suspicions. This leads to less communication and to more labored exchanges, which have as their object obfuscation instead of enlightenment, darkness and shadows instead of brightness and clarity.

Although I said this view that we are ONE is metaphysical, there is some evidence to suggest that it is based on physics. Author Gary Zukav, quoted in Wayne Dyer's book *You'll See It When You Believe It*, says that in quantum mechanics "all of the things in the universe (including us) that appear to exist independently are actually parts of one all-encompassing organic pattern, and . . . no parts of that pattern are ever really separate from it or from each other."

Is it any stretch of the imagination to believe that if we signal openness and clarity to our counterparts, they will do the same?

If there is this link, and I believe there is, then we might go so far as to say by becoming clear ourselves—and this includes becoming personally transparent—we will actually assist others to become clear in turn. Plain talk begets plain talk.

People that tap into this verity are rewarded. One of them that comes to mind is best-selling author Joe Girard, the self-proclaimed world's greatest car salesman. If you read his book *How to Sell Anything to Anybody*, you'll learn exactly how he creates identification with his clients, motivating them to select and prefer him as their car source. Girard's pitch is utterly simple and clear: "I'm like you, and you're like me. So, why not get a car from someone who is just like you?"

Does that appeal work? Is this really what he says? I invite you to read his book for yourself, because he offers some very good, ultrabasic, practical insights into human nature. But for our purposes, let me repeat our point: we are one and the same. At least this is a thesis I'd like you to entertain as you prepare to speak or to write.

Chapter Two

The Art of Preparing
Crystal clear Messages

Robert Maynard Hutchins, the esteemed former head of the University of Chicago, once said the true test of someone's knowledge isn't determined by how many facts are at that person's command. Rather it is how a person commands the facts he has at hand, how he organizes and structures them.

You might expect such a remark from a university president. Institutions of higher education are bastions of organization, beehives of departments, disciplines, and divisions.

One of my PhD advisors counseled us on the importance of defending our intellectual turf from poachers. He said during our careers we'd be called on to defend and determine where our field—communications—began, and others, such as psychology and other social sciences left off. He partly addressed that challenge for us when he pointed out that our field is concerned with how messages link people. In this chapter, we are going to focus on creating the best messages—ones that are constructed sturdily, creating credibility and clarity.

If you are developing a speech, how should you organize it so it will convey your ideas in a logical, easy-to-remember way? If you are writing a memo, how many main points should it contain? Is there a natural limit, or one that experience has determined that we should follow as a rule of thumb? What if you're in business and a prospective client challenges you with this question, as I heard it early in my consulting career: "Why should we do business with you instead of with the person down the street?"

I wasn't 100 percent prepared with an answer to that query, but I was 100 percent prepared with the structure, with the requirements for how I had to marshal my ideas on the spot, and I'm going to share that with you. Before I do, let me address the question that I just raised. Is there a natural limit to the number of ideas we can get across clearly in a written or spoken communication?

Yes, there is.

The limit is THREE. (Very rarely, four, but only if you absolutely, positively need the extra point.)

This is what I call the Rule of Three: In any written or spoken communication, where you have latitude in the number of points you can attempt to convey, make it three or less!

Why? Why three and not five or twenty-five?

Imagine you want to get people to go out and to vote: that is your platform, your main message:

You should get out and vote!

Why?

You might agree with me that it is one of the blessings of a democracy that you *can* vote, that it is your constitutional right.

You might also agree that every vote counts, and as we saw in a recent presidential campaign in the United States, the difference in the ultimate tally was just a few thousand ballots out of tens of millions cast. A senatorial contest in Minnesota, which involved a lengthy but necessary recount, was won with a few hundred votes. A mayoral candidate recently lost an election by a single vote. He failed to cast a ballot for himself!

You might also agree with me that if you dislike an elected politician's conduct, yet you didn't make the effort to vote for his or her opponent (or to run your office yourself), then you might be better advised to blame the person you see in the mirror.

For these reasons then, you and I should get out and vote!

I structured this little oration on the Rule of Three, as you might have noticed, by providing you with three reasons to follow through with my suggestion.

The Rule of Three is like a three-legged table or stool. They will support a platform. So will four legs, for that matter, but often four legs are simply one too many.

Five-legged tables exist too. Many of them are antiques, and I own one, in beautiful golden oak. But that fifth leg is mostly ornamental, and if you or your guests want some legroom, it can be a nuisance.

I understand that during the Middle Ages, preachers used what has been called the Little Method in developing their sermons. They would make a moral point and then go on to support it with three examples drawn from everyday life. Their rationale was that even the most untrained and humble listeners could remember three supports.

But if you go beyond that number as a speaker or as a writer, you risk losing your audience to distraction. Moreover, you might come across as if you are browbeating them. Enough is enough. And how much is enough to create clarity? THREE.

Why not two, or even one, for that matter? Couldn't we formulate a speech that says you should vote and go on to say, "Because if you don't and a bozo gets elected, you'll only have yourself to blame"? That's ultrasimple and to the point, isn't it?

Yes. But there is another dimension to creating clarity (which we will spend more time with in another chapter), and that is CREDIBILITY. To a large extent, our messages will be positively and warmly received based on the credibility we have as speakers and writers in the minds of our audiences.

While there are some aspects that are out of your control—such as your prior reputation or your lack of familiarity to the audience—other elements of your credibility can be enhanced in the message itself.

One of these elements is the message's *authority*: the extent to which it offers proof of its main proposition, and this is based on how you support your message. If you simply offer one or two reasons to support your main point, then your message does not sound so well thought through. Use three, and this makes you more credible.

So when that prospective client asked me, "Why should I select and prefer you?" I replied: "You should select me for these reasons: First, I have a tremendous amount of experience assisting growing enterprises. Second, my training works to significantly increase sales. Third, I am available to start your project right away. For these reasons, you should select me!"

How successful was I in responding to his question?

After he agreed to hire me, I went to his place of business, and he introduced me to his partner. He looked at me and then to his partner and said: "I threw Gary a curve over the phone to see how he would handle it, and he hit it out of the park. I asked why I should hire him, and do you know what he said? I should hire him because he has vast experience, his methods increase sales a bunch, and he's available to start right now. What do you think of that answer?"

I'd like to share with you the best format for applying the Rule of Three that I have ever found. In fact, this is the best format for organizing your ideas clearly that I have ever encountered. It is called the PEP format, and here's how it works:

First, make a MAIN POINT.

Second, SUPPORT YOUR MAIN POINT WITH THREE REASONS.

Third, RESTATE YOUR MAIN POINT.

That's it!

PEP stands for POINT, EVIDENCE, and the restatement of the POINT. If you follow this format in developing speeches and written communications—from emails to memos to client conversations and even sales talks—you'll boost your clarity and credibility in short order.

In fact, I have already used it on you twice.

The first time, I exhorted you to vote. I said: "You should get out and vote!"

Why?

You might agree with me that it is one of the blessings of a democracy that you CAN vote, that it is your constitutional right.

You might also agree that every vote counts, and as we saw in a recent presidential campaign in the United States, the difference in the ultimate tally might be just a few thousand ballots out of tens of millions cast. A senatorial contest in Minnesota, which involved a lengthy but necessary recount, was won with a few hundred votes.

You might also agree with me that if you dislike an elected politician's conduct, yet you didn't make the effort to vote for his or her opponent (or to run your office yourself), then you might be better advised to blame the person you see in the mirror.

For these reasons then, you and I should get out and vote!

That is a PEP-formatted talk in action.

My second unannounced example of the PEP format was the way I replied to that business inquiry. This use was closely cropped, I'm sure you'll agree. I said:

"You should select me for these reasons: First, I have a tremendous amount of experience assisting growing enterprises. Second, my training works to significantly increase sales. Third, I am available to start your project right away. For these reasons, you should select me!"

Isn't that a succinct, clear, and persuasive package?

Why don't I make the previous sentence into a PEP talk, while I'm at it?

You should use the PEP format for three reasons:

It is succinct. It is clear. It is persuasive.

Therefore, you should use the PEP format.

Let's elaborate a little on these methods, shall we? They are even more universal than I have said so far. Specifically, let's look at how this strategy works in the real world, and to do that we only need to listen to countless moms and dads as they inadvertently but quite effectively apply the PEP format to communicating with their kids:

No, you can't go out and play until you have:

1. Finished eating your meal with us;
2. Helped to clear the table; and
3. Put your toys away, where they belong.

After you've done these things, you can go out and play.

I was fortunate enough to be on a team of crack trainers that taught senior U.S. Navy executives to manage by objectives and to implement merit pay for performance. In intensive sessions we trainers were trained to train, even though all of us had extensive prior experience in classrooms and in front of corporate and organizational audiences.

Our Navy trainers taught us to use TCPs, which translates into *three clear points.*

The idea is to preview each learning unit with what we're going to cover. Then, of course, we cover what we said we'd cover. Finally, we end the unit with our TCPs, the three clear points that we hope our listeners will take away from the lecture or discussion.

Military training is famous for following the Rule of Three. Speakers are taught to

1. Tell them where you're going;
2. Go there; and
3. Tell them where you went.

The Brevity Experiment

In speech and writing classes it is commonplace for the instructor to offer a graphic example of how we tend to overexplain.

A typical business letter, consisting of about 250 words, is shown on the screen.

Next to it, the identical letter is displayed. Only this time, every other word has been removed, leaving gaps at each excision.

The discussion leader then asks the class to compare the two, especially paying attention to this question: "Apart from grammar and verbs, are both letters equally comprehensible?"

Generally, students go on (at length) about how eliminating every other word utterly alters the document, making the one that is 50 percent shorter in word count nearly unrecognizable.

Then, after most critics have gone on record excoriating the shorter letter, the instructor explains an experiment that followed this exact procedure, with radically different results.

An experimental group was given the shorter letter to read and then took a comprehension test. It scored somewhere in the 90 percent bracket of understanding. A control group was treated to the entire letter. Not a syllable was missing.

That group took the same comprehension test, and as one might predict, it scored higher than those that saw only 50 percent of the text. But here's what's surprising.

The control group also scored in the 90 percent range—only a few points higher than those that operated with deficient input.

The conclusion: many of our words are unnecessary if mere comprehension is our goal. Speakers and writers repeat themselves, not by plan, but quite by accident.

I've just done the same thing. I wrote, "Not by plan, but quite by accident." Don't those two phrases say more or less the same thing? Couldn't I have stopped myself from blabbing by simply offering the first part—"Not by plan"—or by using the second part—"Quite by accident?"

What's the big deal? you might wonder. *Economy* is the answer. When we speak or write less, we save time in composition. We also save the recipient's time in listening.

But the crucial question presents itself: *does economy always serve the purpose of creating crystal clear communications?*

If this were an equation, we might try to reduce it to this: Are economy and clarity synonymous? If not, can we at least agree that economy promotes clarity?

Unfortunately, the answer isn't clear-cut. Economy promotes clarity *sometimes*. When we're verbose, over-talking, and if we add weasel words and phrases, such as "kind of," then we're muddying comprehension. For example, as an attorney, if I say: "You should kind of avoid doing that," what idea am I really putting across: "You can do it, but I don't suggest it?" or "Don't do that"?

Communicators weasel when they don't want to hurt people's feelings, and when they're noncommittal and don't want to officially say yes or no. But weaseling like this sends anything but a clear signal to the listener.

Novelists are famous for their florid descriptions of scenes and characters, elaborating upon their physical characteristics. Does this promote or preclude coming across clearly? Most readers appreciate the elaboration: it gives them the impression they are inside of the scene and seeing what the characters are seeing. Imagery, and perhaps a lot of it, promotes a clear feeling or a sense of a clear dramatic context for the reader. So for the novelist and her reader, more is more; more words make for greater clarity, and not less.

I read a review of a recent book titled *Cold*. It is about the physics of freezing temperatures and below. The author doesn't merely offer mathematical equations, but he delves into the impact of cold on various species, describing at length how certain birds must eat so much so often so that they can flap their wings sufficiently to stay warm and survive. It's *that* cold outside. By offering us a word picture, he gives us an entirely new appreciation of utterly frigid temperatures.

Previously I mentioned redundancy, which is saying the exact same thing twice or more in a compressed period of time. That definitely seems like overtalking or overwriting, correct? Consequently, it seems wasteful and not at all helpful in promoting clarity.

But, from an effective communication perspective, there is a lot to be said in support of INTENTION-ALLY REPEATING YOURSELF if your goal is to optimize understanding.

We saw how in an experimental context we could excise every other word in a letter and produce roughly similar scores on a comprehension test. But that is a very controlled situation. When we look at comprehension, especially understanding spoken language, will striving help clarity or hurt it?

There's substantial support for the thesis that PURPOSEFUL REDUNDANCY PROMOTES UNDERSTANDING, especially when communicators are interacting through speech.

Language That Rubs You the Wrong Way

I was sitting in the dermatologist's office, waiting to speak to the intake nurse. The bump that bounced me into the place was literally rubbing me the wrong way, making it difficult to sit in my office chair. So as most of us do, I was there in isolation, stimulation starved by the porcelain landscape, rehearsing my story.

We rehearse because we want to accurately convey our symptoms and to save everyone's time. And the clearer we can be, the better.

Yet my cortex wasn't cooperating. Suddenly the word *subcutaneous* popped into mind. That means *under the skin*, which is where the lump in my back was. *Subcutaneou*s is medical talk, and as a communications professional, I have a penchant for using terms relevant to an art or science if I am even remotely conversant with it. More to the point, I have a showoff lurking inside that is always tempted to jump onto all the wrong stages to hog the limelight.

Subcutaneous. "Gee, how can I wedge that polysyllabic power word into a sentence?" I wondered.

Then I stopped myself. "Hold it. Why are you trying to impress, and do you think that word will say you're a smart guy? More like a smart aleck."

In higher education, you get points for using fancy words and for impressing your professors with your verbal acuity. You sound smart, like the kind of individual the teacher sees in the mirror each morning. You're just the sort that gets good grades and goes on to glory in academia, providing cocktail-party bragging rights to the trainers that trained you.

But outside of academic life, especially in America, there is a populist or egalitarian ethos that says you'll be punished if you seem pompous, parading your know-how, credentials, or special abilities.

Returning to earth, I counted syllables. Am I saving any time by substituting one word, *subcutaneous*, for three? *Under the skin* contains four syllables, and *subcutaneous* has five. That one word actually is less economical, in this sense, than stringing together the three everyday words.

Another reason to use the phrase *under the skin* is the fact that no one will misunderstand these words. But it is just possible that the intake nurse won't know the word *subcutaneous* and will potentially be placed in the embarrassing position of admitting as much.

Do I want to make someone squirm? No, I want this pesky bump removed. That's why I'm there, and she's there to help. Why run even the slightest risk of offending her?

Now here's a hoot. The next thought that popped into my mind was, "What if I am wrong about *subcutaneous*, and it means something other than what I think it means? Then I'll have to restate the description of my symptoms, probably inserting the phrase *under the skin* after all. Plus, I will have embarrassed myself!"

But wait! There's more, as they say in those late-night ads on TV.

If I use three words, *under the skin*, and one of them is garbled or the nurse hasn't tuned in for all three, has selectively listened to two of the three, she will probably still be able surmise the gist of my description from the context. She'll know what I'm getting at.

But if I blurt out *subcutaneous*, or fail to articulate it clearly, I'll have to repeat it or she'll carry on, putting notes on the chart, without a clue to what I mean. That's wasteful at best, and hazardous to my health at worst.

What are the points about clarity that this linguistic adventure summons?

1. Smaller words are better than bigger ones, as a general rule. Providing they convey the same meaning, and it doesn't take forever to utter them, you'll be better off using them.

2. Language that is ostentatious, that brings undue attention to itself, causes problems. Listeners end up paying too much attention to *how* you have expressed something instead of your message. Marshall McLuhan famously said, "The medium is the message," but this isn't so when your goal is to express something clearly.

3. Trying to seem smart, a cut above, distinctive, is rewarded in some circles, but not outside of them. Poet E.E. Cummings used an odd format, placing words and phrases at unusual spots on the page. He also used lower-case print, sometimes signing his name "e.e. cummings." Bending and reshaping language are perfectly proper poetic tools, but they are probably out of place in the corporate boardroom or in a business memo.

Chapter Three

Secrets of Appealing
to Any Listener or Reader

I taught public speaking, rhetoric, and a number of other communication courses at the college level for over five years, and yet I do not recall coming across a chapter in any major book dedicated to asking questions. Yet how else can we know, with any degree of clarity or certainty, about the feelings, facts, and ideas that our listeners and readers are fostering?

Lots of titles teach advocacy and debate, persuasion, and influencing skills, yet they ignore one of the most vital ways of subtly aligning others' interests with ours.

Until recently, the great majority of books and other resources in the area of selling failed to broach the topic of asking questions, yet is there a more direct way of appealing to the needs and wants of potential customers?

Few customer-service texts cover the topic, unless they are discussing survey research. Yet is there a better way of finding out how patrons in a restaurant are responding to the fare than by asking, "How is your meal?" One of my law professors, who was instrumental in helping the Subway sandwich company thrive, noted, "You'll never make it as a manager in the restaurant business unless you're comfortable walking up to diners and asking them, 'How is everything?'"

Zen Buddhists are famous for saying that the best way to communicate with another being is through direct pointing. No speech is required when we suddenly see something breathtaking along a hiking trail or off in the distance. Pointing says it all.

Direct asking is just as powerful when we need to learn, when we're seeking guidance, and when we hope to understand one another.

The philosopher Socrates was famous for creating crystal clarity among his students not by telling them things, but by asking superior questions that guided them to certain principles. Law schools and some business schools use the same format, employing a case method to elucidate pertinent points through poignant probes.

The Bible says in one of its most quoted passages: "Ask and it will be given to you; seek and you will find; knock, and it will be opened to you" (Matthew 7:7).

Asking is empowering both to the one doing it and to the one that is called upon to respond. Providing, that is, that the questions are authentic and more than rhetorical, uttered for their own sake, or merely perfunctory.

It is hard to mention customer service without referring to an instrument that asks a lot of questions: the survey. Surveys are often engineered to provide answers that are only "good and better," and not the truth. They are much like the server in a restaurant who hastily hands you the check and asks, "Can I get you anything else?" The timing of the question belies its sincerity. If the check has already been calculated, that server is really saying: "This meal is over!" and "Please clear the premises so I can seat the next entrée eater!" In this context, the question is intended to convey the direct opposite of "I'm ready, willing, and delighted to get you some dessert and coffee!"

How would we improve on this question if we wanted to make it more nearly perfect? We would design it with what I call the three T's: The right *text*, *tone*, and *timing*.

The server's question could sound a little more expansive and generous, so in terms of text, I'd modify "Can I get you anything else?"

"And is there anything else I can get for you?" is an improvement. First, it sounds less abrupt, because it starts with a "more" word: *and*. As soon as you hear it, *and* suggests that there is more of a message or a question to come.

"Is there anything else I can get for you?" is a reminder that, as McDonald's once said in a wildly successful advertising campaign, "We do it all for you." It sends a nifty relationship message.

The next element in delivering our question is using the proper tone. In this case, the best tonal technique is to stair-step, making each word sound as if it ascends to the next.

"And is there anything else I can get for you?" climbs up no fewer than ten tonal steps—one unique tone after the next. This is a lot like singing, and for a very good reason. By rising with our voices, we send a metamessage, a message that accompanies and reinforces the text. That message is: "And I really want to do it for you!" So, we're explicitly saying, "And is there anything else I can get for you?" while elevating it, turbocharging the message with a tonal booster.

Then there is the timing component. To seem sincere, we cannot be repudiating our message at the same time we're delivering it. So we shouldn't rush through the text, even if we are in a hurry to get to the next table or transaction. The timing has to reinforce the idea "Take your time!" and to do that, *we* must take our time in saying it. As I noted, we shouldn't drop the check before finding out if we can be of further assistance, because this nonverbally cancels the verbal message.

As a communication rule of thumb, and I'd like you to make a special note of this, WHEN THE VERBAL AND NONVERBAL MESSAGES FIGHT EACH OTHER, THE NONVERBAL WINS!

So by physically dropping the check, the waiter declares, "Meal over!" while her text about getting something else says, "Meal continues!" Which one wins? "Meal over!"

But if we say those words I substituted—"and is there anything else I can get for you?"—what would happen if our tone went down instead of stair-stepping, as I advised? We'd also be sending a mixed message, one with our text and its opposite with our tone. The tonal message would say: "I don't want this meal to continue, and you don't really want anything else, do you?"

Experiment with text and tone blending on your own. Utter aloud the question we have been using so far: "And is there anything else I can get for you?"

The first time, stair-step upwards. The second time, descend, going downward on each successive word.

Which rendering sounds more sincere and more helpful, and above all is a *more clear-cut* question?

I'm sure you'll agree that it is when our tones move *up*.

One more thing: when we go down the stairs tonally, we tend to sound sarcastic. As a message strategy, this might be a success for stand-up comedians, but it promotes misunderstandings and complications for the rest of us. Sarcasm in effect says, "Don't believe my text; believe my tone instead." If I ask you, "How do I look?" and you reply, "You look great," I should be able to interpret that as a compliment, correct?

And I will, if your tone goes up. But if your tone descends on each word, or even sounds flat, then I'll interpret your reply as sarcasm, and I'll think you're insulting me, making a joke about my appearance.

Some people inadvertently sound sarcastic, thus sending mixed messages when they don't intend to. As a result, their sincerity is held in question, and they cause needless complications in their lives.

Sarcastic people can also get into a lot of trouble when they communicate in writing, especially through email. The challenge they face is that tone is silent in written media, so all that readers have is text, and taken by itself, that can send the opposite message of what the writer wishes to convey.

Certain punctuation forms have been created in order to come to the rescue, such as the semicolon and close parenthesis typed together, which resemble a wink: ;), or using emojis. But as a rule, these are not used in serious communications. Besides, it is a better practice to create clarity, which creates as few complications as possible.

Our clear point so far is this: if you want to formulate a perfect question, make sure that the TEXT, TONE, and TIMING are in perfect alignment, that they are reinforcing and not repudiating each other.

There are three general rules for forming perfect questions. Generally, they should be (1) brief and (2) friendly and (3) should elicit a quality response.

Let me give you an example of a perfect question that I devised when I persuaded some forty universities to sponsor my seminars. After I introduced myself and mentioned that I had developed a popular program, I said:

"I was wondering how might we pursue the prospect of bringing it to your campus?"

Let's see if it holds up to the three-part test.

1. Is it brief? I believe it is as brief as it can be without seeming too presumptuous or curt.

2. Is it friendly? I believe it is by its use of the "we" word and the phrase "pursue the prospect of bringing it to your campus." I didn't ask, "Can we do this course

there?" "Pursuing the prospect" of doing it there was a more delicate and less commitment-seeking way of broaching the subject.

3. Did the question elicit a quality result? Yes. With uncanny regularity, I was asked a series of questions in response, such as "Can you send me something to look over?" and "What are your compensation requirements?" In almost every case, I was asked friendly questions in turn, which moved us very close very quickly to a commitment to doing the class.

Sometimes one perfect question will dovetail nicely into the next.

When I was asked, "Can you send me something?" I'd respond with, "I'll be happy to, and if everything is in order and you like what you see, what will be the next step?"

I built this into my conversations for several reasons. First, it saved time, because if I mailed my materials, it could have easily taken an additional week to advance the program: I'd have to wait for the material to be received and to be discussed and digested, and then I'd have to make a follow-up call that actually reached the decision maker. By implying that "everything will be in order" and "you'll like what you see," I reached the next hurdle in record time.

Typically my counterparts would reply, "Well, then, I think all we'd need to do is discuss possible dates and compensation," which we'd cover in that same initial conversation.

Not all attempts at using perfect questions end well or accomplish the goal.

For instance, I was hoping to do a project with a company that manufactures and distributes calendars and calendaring software. When the president got around to asking me how I organize my life, he mentioned his products and quipped, "What's the alternative to using them?"

Let's apply the three-pronged test to his question.

1. Is it brief? Yes, it is.

2. Is it friendly? No, it isn't. It's a direct challenge, superior-sounding. That type of query evokes a counterchallenge and conflict, which is not helpful if we want to sell our ideas, ourselves, our products, or our services.

3. It did not lead to a quality response, because I simply bit my tongue instead of rising to the bait by saying, "I like my organizational scheme very much, no thanks to you!"

I have built sales campaigns almost entirely around perfect questions. In helping a company that specializes in counseling college-bound students about where to seek loans, grants, and scholarships, I sequenced a series of three questions for the parents:

1. Where is William thinking of attending college?

2. About how much do you think that is going to cost each year?

3. If we could show you some sources for obtaining grants, loans, and scholarships, would you find that helpful?

Here are the typical replies we heard:

1. He's going to State.
2. More than we can afford; that's for sure!
3. You bet! What do you have?

So far this is a perfect conversation, and here's why. We were able to establish that our prospects had a genuine need, we got them to express that unmet need, and, crucially, we motivated them to ask for our help in addressing their need.

This, by the way, is the ultimate in what is often called *consultative selling*.

It depends on the deft deployment of perfect questions, though few deliberate practitioners of consultative selling are capable at crafting them—much less capable, may I say, than you will be!

Traditional selling, by comparison, depends on *telling* rather than *asking*.

Do you think we could have just as easily *told* our way to a positive outcome?

"We show parents of college-bound seniors various sources for grants, loans, and scholarships, and we'd like you to consider using our counseling service, OK?"

Would that have worked as well? Would it have been nearly as gently persuasive?

What we know about selling is this: when people feel they are being sold, they rebel against the attempt. They eschew obvious manipulation and messengers that seem strategic.

There is an adage that is worth remembering: PEO-PLE HATE TO BE SOLD BUT LOVE TO BUY! This seems paradoxical, but it isn't when you consider the art of asking perfect questions.

Well-constructed questions empower people to purchase and to feel completely in charge of conversational outcomes. But if you hit them over the head with what you want them to hear, retaining control for yourself by making assertion after assertion, and they'll run away from the talkathon.

How do you know when you have asked a perfect question? What are some of the signs?

One sign is when people reply with a smile, "That's a good question!" and then they try their best to address it.

Peter F. Drucker was called "the man who invented management" by *Business Week* magazine. Singing his praises in remembrance of him, former General Electric CEO Jack Welch remarked that Drucker had an uncanny ability to ask a question or two that would open the eyes of senior management. Specifically, he asked Welch, who presided over a conglomerate of vastly dissimilar businesses: "If you had it to do over again, would you enter these businesses today?"

That single question encouraged Welch to issue an edict: every GE company had to rank number one or two in its industry, or it would be either improved or sold.

Drucker's question was "perfect" and meets all of our criteria:

1. It was simple.
2. It was friendly.

3. It led to a high-quality response, in this case to the reappraisal and reengineering of the world's largest conglomerate.

Do you think Drucker would have been nearly as effective had he stated: "You know, you'd probably never enter most of these businesses today, so I suggest you sell them off if you can't turn them around right away."

Telling in this manner would have resulted in a defensive response of "No sale!"

Asking made all the difference and changed the lives, careers, and fortunes of hundreds of thousands, perhaps millions, of people.

Let's bring this down to a family perspective. Marshall Field was a legendary retailer at the time my dad was growing up in Chicago. Thinking that he might want to pursue a military career, my grandfather sat him down for a chat, and asked him a simple question: "Which would you rather be: a field marshal or a Marshall Field?"

You should have seen my dad's eyes light up and mist over when he shared that question with me decades later. He chose to go into business, and I think he was pleased with that decision. He was always deeply enamored of the question as well as with his father's wisdom in asking it, especially of a headstrong young man, his son.

Remember: asking perfect questions is another audience-friendly and listener-friendly way of creating clarity.

The Importance of Listening

Some wise person once remarked, "It doesn't do you any good to keep on talking if nobody is listening."

According to one statistic I read, 50 percent of what we hear is never processed consciously. It's going in one ear and out the other.

Any schoolteacher that has faced an unruly, raucous bunch of kids would vigorously concur. If you're the parent of screaming, fit-throwing toddlers, you have undoubtedly reached the same conclusion. Much of the time those that need to listen aren't doing so.

To be effective and to fulfill his purposes, a talker needs to interact with a capable, undistracted listener. But in the hustle and bustle of this multitasking milieu in which we work and live, getting someone's undivided attention even for a few seconds is a lot to ask.

This is especially the case because when we speak, we are facing four types of problem listeners: *selective, insulated, defensive*, and *ambushers*. We're going to discuss them in detail, noting how to overcome the challenges they present to getting your messages through to them clearly.

The *selective* listener hears only those remarks of obvious interest to himself. When we are talking about him and only about him and his interests, we have rapt attention.

The *insulated* listener tunes in only for comments of obvious interest to him or her. When you're talking about them explicitly, they're with you, but you can hear them fading away when you discuss anybody or anything else.

You can hook them back into the chat by using "you" messages, starting with "As you know," "As you'd appreciate," and "I'm sure this has happened to you." You can also use their name, but don't overuse it, or it will sound gimmicky.

The *defensive* listener takes practically everything said as a personal attack.

"How are you today?"

"I wonder what he meant by that!" he thinks.

Six types of message cause defensiveness: ones involving *evaluation*, *control*, *strategy*, *neutrality*, *superiority*, and *certainty*. Steer clear of them. Instead try to use the supportive six: *description*, *problem and solution orientation*, *empathy*, *equality*, and *flexibility*.

The *ambusher* is waiting to attack your position, having taken umbrage with something you said long ago. It reminds me of story about early movie comic W.C. Fields, a well-known carouser who was on his deathbed when a reporter noticed him reading a Bible.

"Have you got religion suddenly?" the journalist asked.

"Nope," Fields replied, "Looking for loopholes."

This is what ambushers are listening for as you talk. If you suspect you're speaking to one, simply ask, "Is there anything questionable about what I'm saying?" or "Do you have any questions?" That should smoke them out.

In addition to problem listeners, there are environmental obstacles that can prevent us from transmitting crystal clear messages, such as noise. Do what you can to take charge of the environment, whatever it is, so your message doesn't have to compete with distractions.

Just remember this: A key way of appealing to any listener is to become one yourself!

Metamessages and Relationships

There was a Neil Diamond song long ago that was a favorite of one of my intimates: "You Don't Bring Me Flowers." It's a sad tune, and it wasn't actually true in my case, but she liked it anyway, as depressing as I found it. There's no accounting for taste, right?

But that song title is bursting with meanings. Specifically it says, "I know something has changed. Our relationship isn't quite the same."

When communicating, as I've already pointed out, your text sends a particular message, but your tone and timing might put that text into doubt, or repudiate it.

If I say, "I like you!" taken at face value, it seems to send a crystal clear message. But if I say it with a declining tone, I might be adding a huge BUT to that positive sentiment. "I like you, but you are starting to get on my nerves" might be the complete message that I transmit. It its totality, it's a mixed message, which is inherently confusing. But in the real world, we're sending mixed and inconsistent messages all the time, aren't we?

I'd like to look at that third T that I mentioned: timing.

I've been trying to play matchmaker between a colleague who is a professional speaker and another consulting firm. The firm has retained me to conduct some seminars at an international conference, and they asked me if I knew some top-notch associates that might add value to the overall conference.

I've been trying to put them together, but there have been some silences that have occurred that could skew our relationships. So I've made a special point of keeping my colleague in the loop regarding our overall progress. This has taken the form of sending emails that say, "I'm still not sure about X, but I'll keep you posted." And that's what I've done through irregular but frequent updates. If I've said, "I should know this by Friday," yet I don't actually get that information, I'll communicate this fact as soon as I *don't* know.

Why am I going to such trouble? Because I appreciate a slogan that is popular in these contexts: You cannot *not* communicate.

For instance, let's say that Friday I mentioned came and passed by without an email from me to my colleague. Would I have *not* communicated? Most folks would say yes. Not sending something at that time is synonymous with not communicating.

But in our guts and psyches, we know that failing to communicate *is* a form of communication—it arouses a meaning. That meaning could be, "He doesn't care about me," or "I suppose the deal is threatened, or it has fallen through," or perhaps "Maybe getting in touch slipped his mind." Very possibly, the meaning that might be attached is "I guess he didn't get the facts he thought he'd have at this point, so he's waiting until they come in."

There are many negative construals that can be affixed to my behavior if I do not expressly communicate. I understand that when the roles are reversed and I'm in my colleague's situation, suffer during a weekend that follows such a silent Friday. So I make a special point of staying on top of the matter by sending as many messages that will keep people enlightened.

In this case, timing, like tone, sends a metamessage, an additional relationship signal to the other person that says:

1. You still matter to me and hang tight for more news; or
2. Things are changing for the worse; or
3. The deal is off and either I'm not going to inform you or I will only if you bother me about it.

Which metamessage do you want to send?

We hear a lot about sustainability these days when it comes to utilizing natural resources. The idea is that renewable resources are preferable than ones that will become depleted. Also, those energy sources that burn cleanly are better for the environment than dirty alternatives.

Are you SUSTAINING your business and interpersonal relationships through sufficiently frequent messages? Exactly what messages are you sending?

Clean up this act and you'll sustain good relations while avoiding the "endangered relationship" list.

Explanations, Long and Short

You may have heard this expression regarding brevity: "We should make things as simple as they can be, but not simpler." If we struggle to condense too much to save time, to cut corners, we'll invariably confuse our listeners or create needless complexity. Or as I'm sure you've heard it said, a shortcut can be defined as the longest path between two points.

I was doing some consulting in Northern California for a distribution company that warehouses and ships hundreds of items. As part of the windup to a call, customer-service reps would inform buyers about when they can expect delivery and the package-delivery service they'll be using. One rep, a very cheerful and upbeat lady, would conclude her calls this way:

"Now your order will be going out YOU PEE and arrive in five to seven business days, which at this point looks like the twentieth of the month, and the total on that will be $275.25, and is there anything else I can help you with?"

"I'm sorry," many buyers would say. "Could you repeat that for me?"

"Sure, I'll be happy to." And she would repeat: "Now your order will be going out YOU PEE and arrive in five to seven business days, which at this point looks like the twentieth of the month, and the total on that will be $275.25, and is there anything else I can help you with?"

Did you catch the odd abbreviation that was being inserted, the one that was compelling listeners to ask for clarification?

Yes, that part: "Your order will be going out YOU PEE." Some would ask outright, "What's YOU PEE?"

"Oh," the helpful rep would reply, "United Parcel Service."

"Ah, UPS," relieved customers would reply.

I kid you not. This was the CSR's standard order-confirmation patter. She made up her own abbreviation for that shipping firm. Admittedly it was one-third shorter, which in this case was one syllable shorter, but in practice it was anything but an economy device. It compelled people to seek clarification on call after call, which takes time, gobbling up precious resources all around. You might say the rep was being creative in inventing her own abbreviation, but it constituted a secret language that erected a barrier to crystal clear understanding.

I've just done something on purpose: I used a common abbreviation, and I'm sure some of you understood it, yet others might have been mystified. I wrote "CSR," which stands for *customer-service representative*. If my usage of that abbreviation gave you the slightest concern that you had missed something and if you invested even a few seconds pondering what *CSR* meant, then you had a first-hand experience with the confusion that this rep created for her customers.

Which brings up a larger point. If we want to communicate crystal clearly, we need to avoid jargon that might be confusing. Lots of occupations have their secret languages consisting of arcane words and phrases and abbreviations that are difficult to decode.

I was driving along California's Pacific Coast Highway on a beautiful Sunday afternoon a few weeks ago when I noticed at the top of the speedometer the digital letters CDS T1.

"Oh, no," I thought. "Do I need some kind of mechanical service, and do I need it now? It's Sunday, for gosh sakes. How am I going to find a dealership that can decode this mysterious malady?"

Then my mind went into overdrive. "What in the world could CDS T1 mean?" I asked myself.

I'm going to let you in on a little secret. I have a technical brain that kicks into gear whenever it is presented with a mystery or a puzzle. I'll sleep on a problem until the answer appears.

Well, I was very much awake at the wheel, but was dangerously sneaking peeks at that display: CDS T1.

"Carbon dioxide SOMETHING?" I wondered, worrying about my two toddlers in the rear seat. "Are we breathing escaped gases?

"Carbon-dioxide system, that's it," I thought. "T1 must mean *trouble 1*, so this is really serious.

"Calm yourself down," I said, utterly missing the ocean's passing beauty on the left.

"What else could it mean?" and just as quickly, the display changed to "CDS T2."

"Is this getting better or worse?" I wondered. "Is this like DEFCON 1 and DEFCON 2?" You know: the military's defense-condition levels that culminate in DEF-CON 5, all-out war.

Was my dash about to go nuclear?

Then it hit me. How utterly dumb I felt.

CDS meant *CD system*, as in *compact-disc system*. *T1* meant *track 1*, and *T2* meant *track 2*.

That secret message was telling me my music was playing, as it should, through the CD system. What did the engineer have in mind when he programmed the dashboard electronics?

I realize this has been a long way to go, but I want to drive home the point (pun intended). Don't use jargon that gets people off message, that confuses them and makes them feel there is an in-group that is in the know and an out-group that is kept in the dark. If there is any chance of confusing with your abbreviations, then please spell out their meanings instead.

Again, try to make things as simple as they can be, but certainly not any simpler!

Grammar and Pronunciation

Grammar teaches us the rules of language. Somewhere in elementary school, a language teacher probably treated you to a number of lectures on the topic that may have resulted in the dreaded diagramming of sentences. You were instructed in the finer points of usage and advised, for example, that *he don't* isn't grammatical and that *he doesn't* is the proper construction.

This is called subject-verb agreement. The subject, *he*, is singular; there is only one *he* to whom we're referring. So, we say *he doesn't* for the same reason we would say *it doesn't*. It refers to a singular entity. *They don't* is proper usage for plurals, when we're referring to multiple subjects.

You're probably familiar with this rule and abide by it without my prodding. So why do I bring it up? Is there a genuine danger that someone will misunderstand the meaning of the declarative statement *he don't go to school*?

I doubt it, but using correct grammar is important for at least a few reasons:

1. If we don't, we'll sound more ignorant than we probably are.
2. We'll lose credibility instantly.
3. Listeners will carom off into distraction, suddenly paying more attention to the mechanics of our sentence construction than to our content.

Therefore it pays to brush up on your grammar if you suspect it isn't as proper as it should be.

Having said that, I should offer an elaboration. There are some grammatical rules that you might choose to violate because you're communicating with a person who breaks so many of them. By sounding overly proper, you might come off as haughty or otherwise odd to him. Perhaps he might think that *your* usage is out of whack.

Some rules are also not widely known or observed. For instance, I might say: "You know what I'm referring to," and this would sound acceptable, correct? But from a grammatical standpoint, it is less than perfect. The rule tells me I shouldn't end a sentence with a preposition. Instead I should say: "You know that to which I am referring."

Let's compare these sentences: "You know what I'm referring to" and "You know that to which I'm referring." Which one sounds better to you? I'll bet it's the one that ends with *to*, a preposition.

We need to add another variable: what is the occasion, and who is sitting in your audience or reading your memo or email? The other day I participated in a meeting at UCLA. Everyone in the room was a senior continuing-education teacher or administrator. They all possess advanced degrees, and they are well-spoken. Moreover, I don't think it is an exaggeration to say they take pride in knowing and abiding by the rules of discourse, written and spoken. So I took pains to avoid ending sentences with prepositions, and I hope and trust I didn't violate any other rules.

Let me say I am quite capable of erring. In fact, let's examine that word, shall we?

Erring is the proper word, and not *erroring*. Likewise, we would be correct in saying, "He erred" instead of "He errored."

Here is the kicker: we need to pronounce words correctly as well. The proper pronunciation of *erred* is not *aired*, it is *erred*, as if you were saying *earth*. I learned this from a constitutional-law professor from the University of San Diego.

But please consider this: so few even highly educated folks know this rule of pronunciation that if you say *erred* as *erred* and not as *aired*, you'll be looked upon quite strangely. Your listener will believe you have made a mistake unless you take pains to say, "And I understand the proper pronunciation of that word is *erred*!" But then you're almost doomed to sounding pompous.

I was doing a consulting program in Kansas City, and one of my contacts corrected me.

I said something like, "He had gotten a high score on his evaluations." She admonished me that the sentence should be, "He *got* a good score" or "He *had got* a good score."

"*Gotten* is not a word!" she said with pursed lips. "I know, because my mother was an English teacher!"

Let me make a comment about her observation:

1. *Gotten* is a word. It is the past participle of the verb *to get*.
2. *Got* might be a preferred usage, inasmuch as it is listed before *gotten* in the dictionary definition.
3. She sidetracked our discussion, which had nothing to do with *get*, *got*, or *gotten*.
4. I felt I was being criticized, as if my knuckles had *gotten* rapped with a ruler.

Which can all sound like that great song from the 1930s "Let's Call the Whole Thing Off," by George and Ira Gershwin.

You like *potayto* and I like *potahto*
You like *tomayto* and I like *tomahto*
Potayto, potahto
Tomayto, tomahto
Let's call the whole thing off

Please Use Restraint

Crystal clear communications also involves restraint—deliberately *not* saying wrong or hurtful things. Silence *is* golden, and as our parents admonished, "Say nice things or don't say anything at all."

Easier said than done.

Today I read about a new "service" in Los Angeles. The article, titled "Revenge by Proxy," narrates how two women started a firm called Alibis and Paybacks. When their clients have beefs with local businesses, they paste and nail up flyers in the vicinity that call out the vendors for their purported misdeeds. They have also waged a public notification campaign against an alleged philanderer that has cheated on his spouse and family. The article mentions that the proprietors of Alibis and Paybacks haven't been sued—yet—for their denouncements, which might be construed as libelous. Is their business a positive or negative contribution to society?

For those who seem to have no other means of redress, who are unsophisticated and don't know how to use small-claims courts or access ombudsmen in the media, this seems like a useful alternative, a way of getting a certain amount of "justice" without resorting to violence or a direct confrontation.

But it also makes already mean streets even meaner.

This practice seems to be in keeping with the idea of flaming: posting rants on the Internet against various entities and individuals. Unlike Internet postings, physical flyers can be removed fairly easily. But we have to ask ourselves, now that we have the power to create crystal clear communications, are we going to devote our energies to building bridges or to burning them?

I was reading an article about a former Detroit auto executive who had fallen on hard times and was defaulting on sizeable personal loans. It's one of those "How the mighty have fallen!" stories, and I'm sure others were drawn to it, as I was.

Under a lot of pressure and now notoriety for his personal economic collapse, he was asked by the news agency Reuters to explain how he could have stumbled as he did.

His succinct reply: "No comment. Thanks for your interest."

I like this reply very much, for a few reasons:

1. First, it sends a signal that is crystal clear: he is not explaining; not now.
2. He hasn't succumbed to a siege mentality, fighting the inquiry.
3. In fact, by saying, "Thanks for your interest," he is leaving the conversation on a high note.

That's poise, grace under pressure, and I admire him for exuding these qualities.

But let's delve a little more deeply into that "Thanks for your interest" message, shall we? What does it communicate, and why is it so powerful? Above all, what can we learn from it?

The exec is acknowledging the press's right to ask. As a public person for many years, he realizes the press has also been friendly to him and to his companies, helping them both to sell millions of cars. Though this isn't a happy circumstance—his personal debt burden and financial meltdown—he appears to realize that a sympathetic portrayal just might reach out to helping hands that can extricate him from the quicksand.

There *is* a tomorrow, and a negative, bitter comment can become an albatross.

Above all, by not leaving the request for comment on a negative note, the exec is paving the way to his recovery, which has to begin in his heart and mind. We only poison ourselves by adding to the spiteful stream of pollution that floods the news and online communities.

The medical axiom comes to mind: "First, do no harm." Scan your speech and writing for defensive messages—those barbs that make people recoil from you and your cause. Ask:

Can I make this point without making the person feel I'm criticizing him?

Can I make my message sound more friendly and less clinical, detached, and possibly indifferent or neutral?

Am I using reason or threats in order to persuade?

Am I building up or tearing down?

Psychologist Erich Fromm said, "If we can't be constructive, we must be destructive."

"Don't do things with a twist" is a Buddhist maxim. This means make your point, but don't send an additional message that rubs people the wrong way, that provokes, that says, "I told you so!" or "If we had done this from the beginning, we wouldn't be in this mess!"

Why Clichés Are Used (and Overused)

"Nobody's popping the champagne yet," said a number of Los Angeles Angels players to a *Los Angeles Times* columnist late in the season, though they were closing in fast on a playoff spot.

Sure, ballplayers are superstitious. They're afraid that if they take their eyes off the ball, they'll suddenly slump and be watching championship games instead of playing in them.

This is a common scenario, isn't it, describing the tense atmosphere of September big-league baseball?

What's just as common is how many clichés I used in making my description.

"Nobody's popping the champagne" and "taking their eyes off the ball" are two clichés that I used in as many sentences.

Here is the definition of a cliché from *Merriam-Webster's Collegiate Dictionary*: "1: a trite phrase or expression; also: the idea expressed by it. 2: a hackneyed theme, characterization, or situation 3: something (as a menu item) that has become overly familiar or common-place."

Language and literature teachers warn us about using clichés because they're too convenient, too easily accessed. They tend to discourage originality in thought and expression. These teachers are preparing the next generation of novelists, but they're not getting folks ready to succeed in everyday life, where clichés are the bread and butter of everyday talk.

I said, "Bread and butter." There I go again!

When it comes to using clichés, you could say I've "been there and done that." Oops! There's another one.

If you string them together (yet another one!), they sound irksome and stale. But from my point of view, their occasional use actually helps people communicate clearly as well as quickly.

At the same time, if you can change a cliché slightly, and you can make it sound distinctive and memorable.

Responding to an online discussion the other day about whether social networking is a useful way to sell publications, I said: "Social networking is an elevator that at best goes sideways, often down, and hardly ever up."

I went on to explain that it is a fine peer-to-peer medium, but it is not a great tool for meeting people of higher occupational status that can advance your career or projects. Calling it an "elevator that at best goes side-ways" is memorable, because it engages the visual imag-ination while violating people's expectations about such conveyances.

Is this a cliché? No, but it could become one if it were used frequently enough.

This is a point to remember. A cliché is used, and, according to some, overused precisely because it communicates something in an economical, often funny or ironic way.

To say that your cousin Mortimer isn't the brightest bulb in the tree is to clearly say he faces some gray-matter challenges, doesn't it? Do you really need to elaborate, or will your listener nod knowingly?

Reviewing my last two sentences, I see that I used yet two more clichés: "gray matter" and "nod knowingly."

At Project Gutenberg on the web, I found a book that contains hundreds of phrases that are useful ways of explaining things. In essence, the author has gathered together clichés and offers them as conveniences to be drawn from instead of pariahs to be shunned.

I side with him. If you want to communicate something quickly and clearly, building on a foundation of cultural acceptance, clichés can help. You can only go wrong if you overuse them, bringing undue attention to them as devices.

Transcendental Communication

Let me share something that occurred the other day as I was jogging to my supermarket, which also contains a concession run by an internationally famous coffee company.

As I ran past a barista who was wearing her company's hat with logo, I nodded and said, "Hi." She ignored me, off in her break-time bliss somewhere, not obliged in the least to greet one of her company's more valued patrons. Maybe she didn't recognize me, and she was saving her hellos for proven, real-time, in-your-face customers, folks who will drop small change and larger into her tip box.

Like many workers, she has an on-stage and an off-stage presence, a private personality and a public one—her space and everyone else's. She's not me and I'm not her, and we only have a functional, mercenary relationship. I pay, she serves. Period. And when I stop paying, the transaction ends, along with her service and any duty she feels to communicate with me.

I used to think that that is enough. She's doing exactly what she is paid for, and she's not paid to smile and be friendly all the time, just on company time.

Once upon a time a financial institution came up with a slogan that said, "Good business is personal."

No argument there. We need to engender a feeling that we're dealing with each customer or client or acquaintance as an individual—even when we have hundreds, thousands, or millions of them.

But isn't this barista I mentioned doing her equivalent of personal communication? It just occurs in fits and starts, ending abruptly.

But *personal* may not be good enough. I'm seriously beginning to believe that the best service, the most sustainable experiences and relationships we can create with our customers and our companies, are *transcendental*. They transcend, or rise above, the ordinary.

I've spoken at length about techniques for creating crystal clear communications. I hope I have delivered value that you can apply immediately, with great results.

But now it's time to go beyond, well beyond, behavior. I think if we want a quantum leap in our communication effectiveness, we need to tap the more spiritual dimensions, because most other competitive advantages are merely material, temporal, and doomed to being duplicated by our competitors. One arena in which we are beyond competition is the spiritual or transcendental. Few individuals and companies tread there, because they're afraid of offending those that have particular viewpoints.

Let me talk about the transcendental in two contexts: the martial arts and presentations such as this book.

I invested eight years studying Kenpo Karate, in which I attained the rank of Shodan, first-degree black belt. Though more than 10,000 students passed through my school's portals over its thirty-plus years of existence, I was only the twentieth person to reach black belt.

When I was interviewed as a prospective student, I was asked a trick question: are you seeking physical skills, mental abilities such as discipline and focus, or spiritual development?

I opted for the third, and that spiritual or transcendental part of my training made all the difference. When you advance with the spirit, you're faster, more powerful, and more effective. You anticipate your opponent's moves, and often instead of having to block or strike or kick, you simply take one step away and you're out of range. Most importantly, when you move with the spirit, your energy draws from a different, nonphysical source, so you tire less, while your opponent wipes himself out.

In spiritual terms, MIGHT doesn't make RIGHT. RIGHT makes MIGHT. Ultimately, you get to a level where you understand that most of our adversaries are created in the mind. We're the source of our own problems and happiness, and conquering our baser motives, including the desire to fight, to win, to build our egos, is sweeter than defeating any person.

Albert Einstein asked this question, reportedly remarking that it is the most important one we can address: "Do I live in a friendly universe or in a hostile one?" Whatever your answer, on a spiritual level what you put out is what you'll get back.

It's easy to adopt a bunker mentality in business and in our personal lives. I knew one senior VP at an investment firm who would announce "INCOMING!" when the phone lines opened up each morning.

Let me give you a concrete illustration of leading with the spiritual, as we call using that power of the universe to guide our martial-arts endeavors. Here is what leading with the spiritual means to me as a speaker, consultant, and presenter. Before I give a speech or deliver a seminar or record a training program, in addition to making sure the room is ready, the equipment is working, and my notes are in order, I do one of two things.

I either say a quick prayer, or I forget.

And often I forget that I have forgotten until well after the program has concluded.

Here's more or less my prayer: "Please help me to make this the best presentation ever. Thank you."

Here's what happens. When I pray, my evaluations are higher than when I don't. And the comments are more likely to read "Best presentation ever!" when I have asked for higher help.

The other day I got an email from a client who was asking some detailed questions about an upcoming presentation. The tone of the note seemed strategic as well as practical. Something was wrong, but you had to read between the lines to detect it.

My first impulse was to dismiss the undertone and to focus on the surface structure until I asked this question: What does my client crave? What is he really asking for? When the question was put that way, the answer came easily: "He wants reassurance that all is well, we're on track, and I'm going to deliver a wonderful experience."

I answered his questions in detail, but before doing so, I said "I'm confident this is going to be a first-class experience, and I'm looking forward to it."

He responded enthusiastically, and everything came off without a glitch.

Could you do something similar to saying a prayer before every significant communication encounter?

Do you think it would help you to communicate more clearly and effectively?

How would you feel after each day? And how is that different than how you might go home now?

Let me give you another application of this transcendental perspective.

When I meet someone or communicate for the first time over the phone or email, I try to find something to like in the other person. Once I do, I project this simple message: I LIKE YOU!

A prominent psychologist was asked, "How can I get others to like me?"

"Like them first," he urged.

Crystal clear Articulation

Here is a way to help any listener to listen better.

A bag clerk at the local supermarket has a communication problem. In addition to doing his job, he opens his mouth and marbles spill out. I'm speaking metaphorically, of course. He doesn't actually gargle marbles, but he sounds as if he does. Consequently, he cannot be understood without extraordinary effort on the part of the listener.

What he is failing to do goes under several names, one of which is *articulating*. *Articulating* is defined as "fully forming your words so they are completely comprehensible to a listener of reasonable sensibilities."

To articulate, you need to employ your articulators. They include your lips, your teeth, and your tongue. If any one of these items is lazy and not fully engaged, you'll suffer from poor diction or sloppy speech.

This implies that effort must be used—continuous exertion—to ensure that our words are sounding comprehensible.

The grocery bagger swallows his words, to use a phrase that was a favorite of one speech teacher I knew. This means most of the sound-producing action is occurring in the back of his throat. His lips, teeth, and tongue are barely engaged in delivering his words.

If you were to watch him when he speaks, you would see that his mouth is agape like that of a fish. Excellent articulators almost close their lips in a pucker when they say the words *wood* or *would*. His remain far apart.

Try saying *would* both ways, open-lipped and tightly lipped, and you hear and *feel* the differences.

Let's focus on one word—*articulation*—to dramatize the importance of fully forming your speech.

There are five syllables: (1) *ar*, (2) *ti*, (3) *cu*, (4) *la*, (5) *shun*. Here are the typical faults that we can have in articulating this word.

1. We can swallow the beginning of the word. Instead of pronouncing *ar* as *are*, we could say it as *uh*: *uh-ticulation*. This drops the R.

2. We can merge syllables, dropping sounds. Some people, for example, would say *ar-ti-clay-shun*. The U sound is eliminated.

3. We might swallow the suffix, dropping the very last sound, the N. One technique to help us to remember to sound out the very ends of words is to add another syllable, the *uh* sound. So *articulation* becomes *ar-ticulation-uh*. Preachers are often known to do this regularly so they'll be heard clearly by those in the last pews.

If you have ever been criticized for being hard to understand, sloppy speech or poor articulation may be your problem. It's time to fix it, because you cannot communicate clearly without doing so. Here are some tips:

1. A speedy voice is the enemy of complete articulation, so please SLOW DOWN. You can always accelerate a little later on, after you have repaired this defect.

2. Go especially slowly with long and hard-to-pronounce words and with foreign words.

3. Breathe deeply. This will enable you to have the stamina and breath to carry all of the syllables to the very end, and you won't lose any because you're out of steam.

4. Practice reading into a recorder. This can provide a great instantaneous before-and-after proof of your specific challenges and progress.

5. Remember: many people equate articulation with intelligence. They rate us on the clarity of our diction. If we're sloppy, they deduct IQ points from their informal scoring of our smarts.

Fortunately, articulation is fairly easy to fix unless you suffer from a congenital problem or you stammer. Even these drawbacks can be minimized, as one of my in-laws dramatized.

Having lost his dad in his teens, to support himself and his mom, he went into book sales. He faced customer after customer and absolutely had to conquer his stammering, which he did quite admirably, going on to found and then run several successful companies.

Clear speech is possible for nearly everyone, so make it one of your priorities.

It's simply an intelligent thing to do!

Chapter Four

Special Communication Challenges and Circumstances

There are several special circumstances in which achieving clarity in communications is essential, but two stand out: selling and customer service.

If you are not in business, if you do not work for someone else as an employee, and if you do not buy goods and services on the economy, this section may seem irrelevant.

But who *doesn't* have to sell his ideas, his influence, and himself? And how can we get along in our world if we aren't committed to serving each other, to helping ourselves and others achieve our goals and pursue our interests?

Everyone sells and everyone services, all the time, when you think about it. One of my best-selling books tacitly takes off on this theme: *Selling Skills for the Non-salesperson*. I maintain that we're all sellers; some of us simply do it more deliberately and effectively than others.

In this chapter, we're going to examine two wildly successful, crystal clear sales and service formats that I have devised and popularized.

Coincidentally, each of these formats contains a ultrasimple four-part sequence. They have been tested and refined in millions upon millions of successful sales and service experiences.

While you can use these methods right out of the box, without adding anything to the recipe, I want to make a larger point about them. Though I'm going to give you sufficient detail to employ them right away, it's even more important for learning purposes to appreciate these patterns as indicating how you can fashion your own.

Who knows? You may come up with brilliant, crystal clear ways to sell, to service, and more, on your own, merely by studying the templates I'm about to give you. That would be great.

Plus, all of us are consumers. We buy things—luxuries and necessities—and we deserve to be treated well or at least fairly. So in this chapter you'll learn some tips for getting satisfaction, and, when necessary, for complaining and winning by sending crystal clear messages and by resending them when necessary.

I'm Not Shopping Here

My local supermarket is part of a huge chain, and I need to disclose straightaway that they trained me as a retail clerk when I was in college.

One torturous week of intensive indoctrination helped to forge me into the customer-service champion I am—at least partly.

They taught me the that company guarantees *everything* it sells, period. That dedication to customer satisfaction has helped it to become and remain an icon in a competitive field.

So when the DVD kiosk at the market was broken, I strode up to the customer-service desk and started to return my rental to the clerk.

"Oh, no, I can't take that. You'll need to call an 800 number. We have nothing to do with that rental company!" She couldn't spew it out fast enough.

"Oh, yes, you can!" I replied in direct contradiction, having done this once before and knowing if that store puts that DVD into commerce, it is to some extent responsible. Plus, knowing the chain's overarching satisfaction policy, I wasn't to be dissuaded from my purpose.

"That's not customer service!" I barked out.

Just as quickly she caved and said bitterly, "OK, give it to me!"

"What's your name?" I asked.

She told me and then added, "Go ahead, complain about me. I don't care!"

Originally I wasn't about to waste any more time complaining, but she convinced me otherwise. I found the manager and said slowly and clearly, "I'm not shopping here today!"

"Why?" he replied, recognizing me as a regular that stops in during his morning jog and at other times.

"Ask so-and-so," I said, and with that I left to do my shopping at another store.

Most companies lose business and never realize it because customers vote with their feet. We march off to a competitor without voicing our complaints. I am resolved to do the opposite—not only to say it once but to retell the story time after time in order to drive home the true costs of customer abuse.

Today, finishing my jog, I said to the clerk, "Please tell the manager I'm not shopping here today, and if he asks why, have him ask so-and-so. He'll know what I'm talking about."

"And by the way," I added, "Today is day two of my not shopping here."

As I was leaving, a very nice and capable clerk saw me, and I told her briefly what was going on. Other clerks at their registers stared, with mouths agape. Undoubtedly they'll hear the story, and waves upon waves of impacts will be felt.

I don't know how long I'll keep this up. I may pop in intermittently to say, "Hi, this is day thirty-five of I'm not shopping here!"

For better treatment, send a crystal clear message of dissatisfaction, which they won't hear if you silently go to a competitor or fill out a survey that is slanted only to say their service is good and better.

And then resend that message, telling them YOU ARE STAYING AWAY!

You'll do more to reform their ways than an individual patron has ever done before.

The Call Path

We haven't spoken much about communicating by telephone, yet it is a medium that is often used to perform customer service as well as sales. Because the telephone is a two-way, real-time interactive medium, it has efficiencies and possible positive impacts that the Internet and email cannot achieve.

I was invited to consult for a mutual-fund company that was ranked almost at the bottom of its peer group—at number twenty-four in a field of twenty-six. The chairman asked me to fix matters and to figure out a way of achieving heightened satisfaction.

We did. In fact, the first year our program was in place, the company soared to number four in the rankings. The following year it reached number one, going "from worst to first," as its president beamed to *The Wall Street Journal*.

In this section I'm going to share with you the crystal clear message I crafted, consisting merely of four lines that helped my client to reach the top.

Lest you think I came up with a mere gimmick, I'd like to share a few details regarding what I did and how I did it. In this way, you might be able to replicate my steps and apply them to your personal and professional challenges.

I started my analysis by defining the end result that we're trying to achieve in our conversations—in this case, customer satisfaction.

When does it occur? How do we know it when we hear it?

I made a decision to track satisfaction as it is expressed within the compass of the call itself, and not to rely on surveys that occur days and weeks later. Customer satisfaction is an *event*: something that is audible and therefore measurable.

My question became, what do satisfied customers do?

Listening to hundreds of calls, I detected that they do three things: (1) they thank representatives in a way that the magnitude of gratitude can be measured; (2) they "sing" back to representatives late in the call, moving their voices into an upper register of joy; and (3) they recommit their business, vowing to come back again.

A great conversation, even if it is a typical account-balance or informational call, can achieve satisfaction fireworks of these types.

The key challenge became this: "How can we persuade customers to do all three by design, with a high degree of regularity?"

Because of time restraints, I've left out some other crucial questions that I asked, but the answer became clear to me. I had to fashion a call path, a partially scripted sequence, to produce customer loyalty.

The Call Path's Four Elements

The call path consists of four elements: a *greeting*, a *promise of help*, *volunteering additional help*, and a *rep's recommitment line*.

"Hello, Goodman Organization, this is Gary, how may I help you?" is the greeting. There's nothing mysterious about its text or timing. But the tone must move up at the end on the word "you."

When the client mentions the reason for her call, the response is: "Sure, I'll be happy to help you with that!"

This sends two messages: you'll get the help you need, and I will enjoy giving it to you. The effect is to relax and assure the person, which tends to make the conversation shorter overall, and filled with less tension and needless chatter.

After we have addressed the customer's question, we volunteer, "And is there anything else I can help you with?" and this elicits a yes or no. Most important, it sends a signal that the call is concluding, and it brings the feelings to a positive point to a crescendo.

Plus it says, "I'm ready, willing, and able to help even more!" which is a very positive sentiment to convey.

Finally, after we have determined there is nothing else to handle in terms of content, we say, "Well, thank you for doing business with us!" or the equivalent.

Typically, this will elicit a "Sure thing!" or "You bet!" or "Anytime!" or even an explicit pledge to return for more purchases. In a word, it produces LOYALTY.

Again, by necessity I have left out a number of bells and whistles and augmentations, especially for dealing well with annoyed or angry folks within the call-path structure. Suffice it to say that there are numerous enhancements.

Here are the results of a properly deployed call path:
1. Conversations tend to get shortened by 20–30 percent, saving time, money, and personnel.

2. Satisfaction scores on external measures soar.

3. More customers than ever follow through on their promises that they're coming back. They buy, again and again.

Recall, if you will, that my client started at number twenty-four out of twenty-six, and then it leaped to number four. Then it got to number one. And then?

The last time I tuned in, it was celebrating its twelfth consecutive first-place finish in customer-satisfaction rankings!

Of course there is value to applying this call path or something similar to your service conversations, on the phone and off. But there is also this clear point I wish to make: the best messages have yet to be invented.

My call path has been used, according to my admittedly imprecise metric, in more than one billion conversations. Yours might be used in even more!

I challenge you to put to use what you've learned here to produce a stunning, crystal clear communication of your own for your specific purposes.

Four Simple Steps to Stunning Sales

How do you make sale after sale?

It's simpler than most people make out.

I was a struggling doctoral student in need of extra cash to pay for a car that I had to buy.

I was already teaching part-time, but that was only lucrative enough to pay for my rent and food. For wheels,

I needed something else, a great supplement, if I could find one.

Sure enough, on the job board at USC I saw a part-time gig at a local office-products company. Flexible hours, it said. They had to be, because I had one of those typical academic schedules that had me straddled between schools and time zones.

In the interview I was asked, "What makes you think you can sell office products?"

"Easy," I replied, "I've been a top salesperson before, and I can do it again." (Some of that was bluster, just so I'd be given a shot.)

I was told to sit next to an experienced pro who was selling to bakeries. In twenty minutes or less, I was asked, "Want to give it a shot?"

I did, but not that salesman's way. Instead I used the four-part formula I'm going to share with you here.

Oh, how did I do?

I made a sale on my first contact, which sent the manager raving to everyone that he had hired a "master!" That job helped me to make my car payments, and then some.

Here is the stunning four-step formula:

1. Opener
2. Description
3. Close
4. Confirmation

I'll briefly explain each step and then pull it all together in an example.

The *opener* is just that. It is a stylized way to begin a sales conversation, a rationale for deserving the attention of the prospect. Although in my books I list ten or more solid openers, for our purposes I'm only going to mention a few. There is the *special-sale approach*, which touts a discount. You can also use the *after-mailing approach*, which refers to something you sent by email or by conventional mail.

This is a good moment to pause to dramatize the power of a good opener.

In a recent online discussion the question was asked: does it pay to send out a direct mailing piece before trying to sell someone?

I had a slightly unconventional slant on this topic, as I think you'll agree.

Let me share an interesting tale with you. A major publisher sent out millions of direct mail pieces. Then it followed up with a call, using the after-mailing approach.

The campaign, which became ongoing, was a huge success. What is especially noteworthy is that the publisher called far more people than the number of mailers it sent out. Let's say it sent out two million brochures. After that, it phoned five times as many people. Clearly the pass-along rate wasn't five-to-one.

When it came time to assess the program's success, there was no material difference in response between people that recalled getting the mailing and those that didn't. Many people simply quipped, "Well, I tend to toss everything of that nature that comes my way," which is to say they may or may not have received it. Their memories were completely unreliable, but this didn't stop the marketers from continuing with their presentations.

"Well, I'm the same way!" they beamed, creating identification and camaraderie. "I round-file a lot of that stuff. Let me bring you up to date. It would have told you about . . ." Typically, the conversations proceeded to a close, and quite often resulted in sales.

The learning point: prior mailings can help to soften resistance to a subsequent sales call. But merely *referring* to the mailer was sufficient to enhance the credibility of the caller and the company, even when the prospect didn't recall seeing the actual brochure.

So we have the special-sales and the after-mailing openers, but there is another one that is at least as powerful. It is the *before-mailing* approach. "I'm going to be sending you a brief article that I think you'll find very helpful in improving your sales," it begins. Then you check the email or conventional mailing address, and you can go on from there.

This brings us to the second of the four parts of the anatomy of a sale: the *description*. There is where you describe the features and benefits of your product or service.

Here is where the famous KISS method applies: "Keep it simple, salesperson!" Introduce two to four features or benefits, and move on. If you overtalk, you'll also raise needless objections and waste everyone's time.

The third part of the sale is the *close*. This is when you ask for the yes. There are three types of closes I recommend, but my favorite is the *assumptive-checkback close*.

"So let's get under way and I'm sure you'll be pleased, OK?"

"Well, the calendar indicates a good time for me to stop by and say hello will be on Tuesday between 2 and 3, OK?"

"All we'll need to get you into this apartment is the first month's rent and an equal amount for the security deposit, fair enough?"

You may have noticed they all sound the same, though they are aimed at slightly different purposes. Each is engineered to produce a quick yes—approval on the spot.

We make an affirmative statement, a decision statement, assuming the yes, and then we check it back to elicit the express approval we need.

The OK is a tie-down that evokes a nearly reflexive agreement, and it is very powerful, so don't leave it, or its equivalent, out of your close.

The fourth part of the sale is the *confirmation*, where we repeat the major terms of the understanding we have reached:

"Fine, just so I'm clear, I'll be stopping by between 2 and 3 on Tuesday, and you're located at 123 Peachtree in Atlanta, is that right? OK, great. I'll see you then!"

Use this simple, clear anatomy of a sale and its four-step sequence, and you'll probably earn more approvals and sales than you ever thought possible!

Revisiting PEP

We've already discussed the PEP format, the three-part structure for organizing our ideas in speech and writing. By way of quick review, PEP stands for POINT-EVIDENCE-POINT.

You may not have realized this, but PEP is an astonishingly simple sales tool. All we do is introduce two words into the formula to make it exceedingly persuasive.

Let say you are explaining the appeal of your coaching services. You might say:

People seek our services for three reasons:

First, they're looking to create a change in their personal or professional lives;

Second, they realize it's easy to get outside help; and

Third, it saves them time, money, and hassles to call on a professional guide.

For these reasons, people seek our services.

That is a neatly informative talk. But is it really persuasive? Not quite yet. By adding two words, we transform PEP into a mighty instrument of motivation. Here's what we do.

Invoke the word SHOULD:

You *should* retain our services for three reasons:

First, we help you to create a change in your personal or professional life;

Second, you'll find it easy to access our help; and

Third, it will save you time, money, and hassles to call on a professional guide.

For these reasons, you should retain our services.

Is this persuasive? Yes and no.

The s*hould* word helps, but what we know from sales experience and from behavioral research is that we shouldn't leave it up to our listeners to seal the deal, to volunteer assent. They need a little nudge to get them off the fence from inaction to action, from sighing to buying.

Again, we're looking for another single word and it's one that you use almost every day. I'm speaking of *OK*.

Just as we used it in concluding our four-step sale, if you tag it onto your PEP point finale, you'll also generate instant assent.

Chapter Five

Staying Positive

At the beginning of this book I mentioned that I am optimistic, which is to say that I believe we can clearly express and get across nearly any point to anyone.

Consequently, I am upbeat and positive about the communication process, believing it is the answer to developing peace and understanding among individuals, families, companies and consumers, and cultures.

If we work hard enough at sharing our ideas clearly, and at understanding other people's, we'll avoid the terrible breakdowns and distractions that inhibit personal growth and world development. These include, on the personal and commercial level, lawsuits, and on the international scene, wars.

In this chapter I'm going to share some of the tools that help me to stay positive about the communication process.

Admire Your Own Work

Let me share a wonderful experience with you.

I was browsing in a bookstore when I spotted a lady perusing business books.

"Wouldn't it be nice if she picked up one of mine?" I thought. Within moments, she did just that, picking up two different titles.

"Please buy them!" was my next thought, not so much for the royalties that would trickle back to me, but for the thrill of seeing a real reader, in the wild, doing what readers do.

Slowly she made her way to the cash register.

"Don't turn back!" I silently pleaded.

I felt like one of those crocodile people on TV, haunting one of nature's obscure locales, spotting a rare species, *librus purchatus*. Purposely I froze, wanting to avoid any moves that might make this most treasured person startle.

Without further ado, she rang them up and departed with them in a nicely creased bag.

"Yes! Yes! Yes! Yes!" I exulted.

This felt like a blissful dream, but I assure you, it actually happened.

Whenever I get stuck and I start succumbing to negativity, I remember this book buyer. I'm not writing just for myself. I'm writing for her, and for hundreds of thousands of people like her.

If you aren't published, or you haven't reached a feeling of total security about your writing, take heart. You may not see others appreciating your output, but you can do it in their place.

Read some of your older writings and admire them as you would a stranger's. Pat yourself on the back, and trust that these creations will find an audience. And if you hang out where readers congregate, you just might witness the audience finding you!

Every Day in Every Way
You're Getting Better and Better!

You might recognize the name Émile Coué. He is one of the granddads of the self-help movement. He worked as a pharmacist in France during the early twentieth century. Coué discovered the power of reciting positive affirmations by affixing brief notes to his prescriptions, describing how the medicines he mixed would help people to restore their health.

After achieving quite astonishing results this way, he coined a single statement that he advised everyone to use that would improve not only their health but their abilities and happiness:

Every day, in every way, I'm getting better and better!

Additionally, he encouraged people to visualize this statement coming true.

Sick people became well, including some that doctors said were beyond help. Sad folks became happier. Nearly everyone Coué touched with his aphorism improved dramatically.

Many have followed in Coué's footsteps, as I am doing now. They particularized his general affirmation, seeking enhancements in specific areas, and you can too.

Every day, in every way, I'm more and more comfortable speaking before groups.

Every day, in every way, my writing becomes clearer and clearer.

Every day, in every way, my confidence grows in my communication abilities.

Every day, in every way, I am achieving understanding and cooperation with other people.

This list is by no means exhaustive, and I encourage you to develop your own.

Or you can simply use Coué's general affirmation:

Every day, in every way, I'm getting better and better!

By the way, you can read Coué's books for yourself for free, at Project Gutenberg, which can be found on the Internet at www.gutenberg.org.

Continue Your Education with Great People

By reading this book you are continuing your education, and I thank you for this. You're giving me this chance to teach, and I'm grateful. We are blessed with countless opportunities to study with wonderful people, polishing our skills in the process.

I was about to board a train from London to Bath, England, when I felt an irrepressible impulse to visit the book kiosk on the platform. I expected the ride to take more than an hour, and I wanted something that would feed my mind.

Staring right at me was a thick paperback titled *Management*. It was the U.K. edition of Peter F. Drucker's classic. I had always meant to read the master in his own words, so this was a moment of serendipity.

As I deciphered the tiny print, I became enthralled. His ideas gave voice to many of my observations as a business consultant. Inasmuch as I had benefited greatly from studying with other luminaries in my academic career, I was driven to see if Mr. Drucker still taught.

He did, at Claremont Graduate University, which named its graduate school of management after him. I studied directly with him for two and a half years, earning my MBA in the process.

I have always contended that there is something special about being in the presence of a great master. It goes beyond mere ego gratification and idol worship. Until I came across a passage in Wayne Dyer's book *The Power of Intention*, I couldn't account for this dynamic.

Dyer describes his encounter with someone that would change his life: the Indian spiritual teacher Mother Meera, who gazed into his eyes, making him feel so energized that he couldn't sleep. Reporting that he himself has had a similar effect on others, Dyer recalls: "I've been told I've had an impact" by "having a meal in a restaurant. I've done nothing. They've felt impacted by the field of high energy we shared."

That's it. Energy that transcended the ordinary made Drucker's classes into great occasions, pilgrimages of executives coming to drink from his deep well of knowledge.

Find the best people in your field and then do what you must to meet them. If possible, have them teach you. It will energize and revitalize your life!

The Smart, the Lucky and the Persistent!

I just finished reading a great article in *The New York Times* about the role gut instinct plays in surviving enemy ambushes in war.

The article says billions are being invested around the world in brain research. Some of that bounty seeks to learn more about how our "second-favorite organ" (as Woody Allen dubbed the cortex) gathers information, particularly that which has survival value.

It occurred to me that intuitive people fall into one category of people that seem to succeed in life: the "lucky." Was it Napoleon or Abe Lincoln who said, "Give me lucky generals" No matter. These leaders felt that luck trumps intelligence, which I see as yet another ticket to succeeding in life. We don't have to look beyond technology and those that invent and exploit it to see that brainy people usually can make a living, though it may or may not be commensurate with their gray-matter endowments.

The third type that succeeds is the plodder, the one who is persistent. A former infantry soldier commented on the *Times* article and sang the praises of these grunts:

"In Combat-The four eyed pencil necked geeks rule, because they work as a team, follow orders, feel responsible for and protective of the other guys in their rifle squad and most importantly-they paid attention during training. They advance thru their fear, surmount real terror and commit great acts of selfless heroism. And they almost never get a medal."

The same poster pointed out that "jocks" and "neighborhood bullies" are some of the fastest to die, because they overestimate their abilities. In other words, their luck runs out, or their intelligence fails to deliver shortcuts.

Unlike their slicker comrades, plodders don't have many delusions to overcome. Not thinking they're smart or lucky, they only do what they know succeeds. They work relentlessly, improving inch by inch. The Cliff Notes lesson on how to survive.

I suppose that is the recipe for spotting land mines or explosive opportunities: inch by inch and not yard by yard.

Try to remember this, and it should help you to stay positive as you seek crystal clarity in your communications.

Being Sensitive to Criticism Isn't All Bad!

Not long ago, my deceased dad spoke to me in a dream.

He recalled the time he produced a TV show in Chicago. The host snickered at him: "Well, nobody can be as perfect as you are, right?"

Bristling from the remark, I recall thinking my dad must have been rebuked in public. "Did he say that on the air?" I asked.

"Yes, he did," my dad winced, still feeling bruised by this episode several decades later.

"Gee, my dad was sensitive to criticism!" I noted, still dreaming.

Then it hit me. "So am I!"

This was far too provocative to pursue in the ether, so I awoke and meditated on this theme in the predawn shadows. I went back and forth with pros and cons. Is sensitivity to criticism such a bad thing?

Yes, I argued. You need a thick skin to get what you can out of life. If you're overly sensitive, nearly any unkind or untrue remark can send you reeling.

Then I reversed gears. But if criticism bothers you, it means you're actually listening to other people, you care about their opinions, and you want to be successful in getting along and working as a team.

Don't we call people that are utterly insensitive and completely callous brutes, outlaws, and sociopaths? Connecting with people is good, and being aware of how you're coming across has survival value.

We need people, and they need us. And criticism can be valuable if we choose to interpret it constructively.

I debated the matter to a stalemate, and when I was finished I didn't know which argument had more merit. I was left with the fact that my dad opened up and shared his feelings about a difficult time in his life, and I commiserated.

Glad I could be there for him!

If you're sensitive to criticism, join the club; you're normal. Just don't take it too seriously.

Actor Jude Law is finishing a stint as Hamlet in, of all places, Denmark. His portrayal will be haunting New York in the coming months for a limited run. Commenting to an interviewer from *The New York Times*, Mr. Law said he doesn't read reviews of his performances. "If you read good reviews," he said, "you become self-conscious about the bits they like, and it starts to make those bits tacky—as if you're churning them out. And if you get bad reviews, they're going to crush your ego. It's like vinegar in the wound. So there's no point in reading them."

His perspective is quite pertinent to me as a writer, teacher, trainer, and professional speaker. I used to bill myself as a top-rated instructor at various university colleges of continuing education. I'm not convinced this self-glorification ever made anyone choose to enroll in one of my courses or to retaining me to speak or to consult for their companies.

Over time, I decided peacocking in this way wasn't all that helpful. I found myself expecting praise and becoming too conservative. I resisted trying out new and potentially ratings-reducing topics.

What did it say about me or about my classes that my ratings were at times flawless, all fives on five-point scales? When I failed to earn the kudos of all, I relentlessly soul-searched to determine how I fell from grace with those few that took issue with my style, content, or treatment.

Were those classes, the ones that failed to reach certain attendees, materially worse than the top-rated ones?

What about the best-selling books I've written, those that have sold hundreds of thousands of copies? Are they more meritorious than the titles orphaned by publishers that were suddenly gobbled up by larger corporate predators just as my tomes reached bookstores?

Now I've come full circle and share Mr. Law's view. I don't really care to see my teaching evaluations or book reviews or to hear feedback unless it is earth-shaking or life-changing. I feel like actors who decline Academy Awards, asking: "How can you compare two artists that do unique interpretations of different characters?"

When teacher A gets great scores for his geometry class, this doesn't necessarily compare to teacher B, who garners glowing comments for his psychology class. In the former case, the bar may be higher, because great geometry teachers are rare; their fields are difficult for students to plow. If we are lucky enough to find a math whiz who is an excellent communicator as well, we're often amazed. Psychology is inherently fun, because it is less exacting and seemingly ALL ABOUT US! Especially for beginners, every session can bring thunderbolts, new insights and revelations, or, as we say in training circles, take-home value. Psychology just might be the closest thing to pure entertainment you can find in a college curriculum, though sociology, a kindred field and one of my near-majors, scores a close second.

Am I in favor of abolishing all teaching evaluations? Not in the least, if only because they are cathartic for the students that fill them in. It makes them feel they have influence, that they are not powerless. They are somewhat like a legislature that can pass nonbinding resolutions. Resolutions are not laws, and while they garner a certain amount of polite respect, they aren't to be taken literally or be pushed too far. Similarly, teaching evaluations and theatrical reviews should be regarded largely as symbolic, opinion-expressing exercises.

In another *New York Times* piece, a professor said students should listen to him "because I know more than you do!" And I'm sure much the same can be said for Mr. Law's knowledge of Hamlet, and for most writers, speakers, and teachers.

Despite the criticism you might receive, continue to speak your mind clearly and convincingly. It will add to your self-respect, and that in itself should help you to stay positive.

Don't Let the Good Be the Enemy of the Get-By

You may have heard the expression "Don't let great be the enemy of good."

That means, more or less, if you have a good job, don't quit in the belief that you can achieve a great job faster by having 100 percent of your time to pursue it. Or if there is a good solution to any problem, don't pass it over because you're convinced a great solution is somewhere down the road.

There's nothing wrong with good. But let's move down the food chain of achievement a little, shall we? Is there something short of good that we're letting good get in the way of?

There is, especially in these economic times. It is called survival, or as sales trainer Zig Ziglar dubbed it, the "get-by."

You might want to live in a palatial home in the hills with a swimming pool and three cars in the garage. That would be great.

Or you might accept a spacious condominium with a lot of nice people living next to and above and below you in a lovely, leafy neighborhood. All of you blissfully share a swimming pool and a nice recreation room.

That would be good.

But in tough times you don't happen to qualify for either of these digs. You are squirreled away in a cramped apartment, with noisy plumbing and gang graffiti a few blocks away.

That's the get-by.

This is still better than what Will Smith's character endured in the film *The Pursuit of Happyness*. If you've seen it, you know what I'm saying.

The key is to keep on keeping on, to hang in there until you can work your way back up the ladder to good, and then if you like, to great.

What's worse than the get-by? It's the BRINK, and that's one place you don't want to be hanging out!

Sometimes you simply have to pull together a talk, a meeting, an interview, or a memo at the last minute. It won't be great, and it may not even be good. It could be a get-by, but that's OK—as long as it's crystal clear!

Staying Positive after Repeated Failures

Have you ever wondered what separates the winners from losers in life?

It isn't that winners lose less often. Babe Ruth held a record for being struck out the most times as well as a record for hitting most home runs. You might say he was the biggest winner and the biggest loser simultaneously.

Obviously, to accomplish both, he couldn't let his euphoria become too extreme or his disappointments grow too severe. Like a warrior, he had to heal his wounds quickly, take victories in stride, and battle on.

In a word, Ruth and all winners, world-beaters, record breakers, must become *impeccable*. Carlos Castaneda was the first to point this out in his books. My impression of an impeccable person is one who is meticulous, who attends to details, does things with care and precision, yet never completely stops in pursuit of a larger objective. This would be someone who deftly applies the law of large numbers (LLN).

LLN folks realize that through the application of repeated attempts at nearly anything, they will ultimately succeed, no matter how long it takes or what flak they have to endure. Once they have a worthwhile goal, they never give up.

Consider the example of Maxcy Filer, who repeatedly failed the quite challenging California bar examination. If memory serves, it took him more than eighteen years to become a licensed attorney. He studied for, and then failed, more than thirty semiannual tests before success came to him.

I met someone who failed the bar exam 80 percent fewer times than Maxcy, before ultimately passing, yet this individual succumbed to a permanent bout of depression.

What is it about Maxcy that made him persist rather than bowing to such prolonged and potentially debilitating results?

Perhaps he is a warrior in the Castaneda mold, an individual who has figured out how to be impeccable in circumstances of unceasing negatives, someone who agrees with Winston Churchill's maxim that "success is the ability to withstand failure after failure and still maintain your enthusiasm."

Castaneda offers hints about impeccability. He says an "impeccable spirit" is the dividend that accrues to someone who "has stored power after tremendous hardships."

This would be a person much like convicted Watergate felon G. Gordon Liddy, who asserted, "Whatever doesn't kill me makes me stronger." How can someone such as Liddy, a bungling burglar, fail so conspicuously and then succeed as he did? As you may know, he went on to a very successful career as an author and talk-radio host.

How do warriors use negative energy to recharge their batteries while others stall at the hint of a setback? Castaneda says, "The trick is in what one emphasizes. We either make ourselves miserable or we make ourselves strong. The amount of work is the same."

Perhaps a vital difference is where one turns one's energy after sustaining a defeat.

Survivors-and-thrivers seem to deflect failure away from them. They don't interpret setbacks as containing nasty messages about their core abilities and their self-worth. For them, failure is, as Henry Ford famously said, "a chance to begin over again."

Martin Seligman, a best-selling author and psychiatrist, has studied happiness in depth. He says resilient people seem to be those that dissociate themselves from failures. They might blame factors beyond their control, but this is a healthy response, asserts Seligman.

For those that fail and stall, it seems to be a different story. They accept blame for what they aren't responsible for. They interpret setbacks as permanent and personal. And they stop or curtail the very activities that, if continued, would eventually propel them to success.

Possibly they won't allow themselves to fail enough.

Staying positive while failing seems a lot like losing and laughing: difficult to do, as well as inappropriate for the occasion.

This isn't required. What *is* required is that we carry on impeccably; that we persist, understanding that failure is no match for a warrior who is committed to soldiering on, who realizes there is no need to fall on his own sword.

Indeed that may be the only and ultimate defeat, the defining characteristic that separates losers from winners.

The Cure for Bad Speech—More Speech!

Aristotle, though a creature of his times, was democratic when it came to the idea of free speech. He was one of the first on record to talk about the marketplace of ideas, indicating that lively give-and-take, or offers and acceptances, would set the value of one's messages and pronouncements, much as the marketplace sets prices for goods and services. The freer the marketplace is, the better the prices and ideas become.

Unshackle yourself. Commit to entering the marketplace every day with your views, your needs, and your skills. Through repeated give-and-take, you'll inevitably improve.

Don't Label Yourself as Smart or Dumb

I'm a fairly competitive guy. So when one of my salespeople challenged me to literally match wits with him, I rose to the bait.

"What's your IQ, Gary?"

"I dunno."

"No, really, what is it? Have you ever been tested?"

"In school I took some exams, and they said I was a classic underachiever, so I suppose they wouldn't bother saying that to a dunce."

"You should have it tested."

"Why, Barry, do I need an IQ test, when my job as a manager is to deal with bozos like you?"

"I just joined Mensa," he went on. "You know, the genius society, and if your IQ is over 130, you can join too! All you have to do is take an IQ test."

This was one of those weird conversations where you don't want to go on with it, but at the same time you can't stop.

"Barry, where would I get an I.Q. test?"

"Mensa will test you, or you could take one at the university. They'll accept that too."

He was right. The counseling center at school administered all kinds of tests, so I could probably get tested for free. Plus, if I turned out to be a certified simpleton, no one would be the wiser but me.

The next week I popped into the center and asked for a test. They said I'd have to see a counselor first. "What a waste!" I thought, but my quest was important enough to slay a dragon or two along the path.

A suitably somber, bespectacled psychologist asked me why I wanted to know my IQ, and I told him about Barry, Mensa, and my longtime personal curiosity.

At the end of our chat he decided to give me, not what I asked for, but a vocational-guidance instrument that informed me I would be great at real-estate sales and would make a very disgruntled forester.

His reason for withholding the IQ test was this: what if I discovered I was a genius? Would I just hang around feeling superior while squandering my gifts? And if I were a dim bulb, what would I do? Would I use this discovery as an excuse to feel inferior and to justify not trying hard to achieve challenging goals?

Having bought into the logic of the counselor, I never bothered to take an IQ test.

Instead I went on to earn five degrees, to teach on the regular faculty at three universities, to teach in continuing education at forty more, and to write some best-selling books.

If my subconscious goal was to prove I was smart, perhaps it would have been more efficient to have found another place to have taken that test.

Anyway, as you may know, tests aren't the ultimate arbiter of IQ. I love a story told by Dr. Wayne Dyer in his book *Real Magic*. He took a test that unwittingly used one of his own writings in the reading-comprehension component. He was marked down because he supposedly failed to properly understand what the author meant.

Study Success and You'll Be Able to Emulate It!

Few things make us feel as positive as the sensation of self-improvement. When we are getting better at something, it creates positive momentum, and we wish to become better still.

One of Peter F. Drucker's recurring refrains was "study success." The idea is simple, really. If we want to know what customers want, observe what they're happily paying for elsewhere, and either imitate that or spin something off that will deliver even greater satisfaction.

The same concept applies to self-improvement and to getting the most productivity from those we manage. We should study who is good at what and ask, "Why?"

Minimally, we should do more of that in which we excel, and if possible, we should analyze what our superstars, our natural leaders and trendsetters, are doing to achieve their exceptional results.

Typically, however, we do the opposite. Instead of promoting and managing strengths, we obsess over weaknesses and miss golden opportunities to build on our successes.

Studying people's success in communicating clearly is easy when you use the Internet. There are countless sources of good and bad writing, for instance, that are entirely free.

I read three major newspapers a day, plus a number of blogs, not cover to cover, but sufficiently. Reading improves my writing, because unconsciously I'm internalizing the structure and content of innumerable authors.

Sometimes I deliberately emulate good writers. For instance, today someone took exception to a comment I made, and I wanted to publish a response, but I thought that above all it should be witty and self-deprecating.

So I asked myself, "How would T.J. Simers respond?" He was a clever sports writer for *The Los Angeles Times*.

And sure enough, I came up with a concise two-liner that made a little fun of me while it made my point.

Study success, and, where appropriate, imitate it. You'll improve your communications and start a positive upward spiral.

How to Conquer Daunting Distractions

When we're trying to get just a little quiet time to compose that important memo or delicately weave together our presentation, we almost always seem to be plagued by devastating distractions that not only sap our energy, but deflect us from our all-important purpose of communication.

Happily, there are ways to conquer daunting distractions. I'll give you an example. In karate, there is a group drill that is done for the benefit of a person we'll call A, who is using his basic footwork to make progress from one side of the mat to the next.

About five people are harassing him, shouting, making jokes about how goofy he looks, razzing him in a zillion ways, and physically pushing him around as well. A's job is to focus on his objective, to keep moving toward it, and to continuously retain his poise and composure while these miscreants are literally and figuratively in his face. It's not easy, but it has universal application.

How many times, at work or at home, have you been pressed by difficult personalities and tasks that just seem to multiply? At some point, you feel overwhelmed, that you can't go on; the distractions are too difficult.

Maybe you need to do some homework for that night class you're taking, and your newborn is crying incessantly. How can you even crack a book when any moment of silence is bound to last no more than a few minutes? Why bother?

At least this is what you're apt to think.

But can you keep your cool enough to make progress, to be a warrior in that situation or in a hundred others that are as vexing?

You can. It's not easy. Here are five things to keep in mind:

1. Not being interrupted is a luxury at any time in our lives. With the reach of cell phones and GPS (global positioning satellite technology), how can anyone cut

the tether and get any peace at all? It's not easy, but most modern people in sophisticated cultures are facing similar stresses. You're not alone. Take comfort in that.

2. You can't be a perfectionist and handle multiple challenges too. With some of your tasks, you'll just have to perform at the get-by level instead of in the upper one-tenth of 1 percent of effectiveness. There is a reason that mom, with three kids going to three different venues after school—soccer, ballet, and the math tutor—has no time to get her hair and nails done.

3. Be like the novelist who finishes a book in a year by writing only one page per day. Break down major objectives into tiny increments. Remember the adage: "Inch by inch is a cinch. Yard by yard is hard!"

4. Don't depress yourself with memories of how easy it used to be when life was simpler. It only seems simpler in the rearview mirror. The good news is you've faced big challenges before and you've succeeded. Don't doubt your abilities to do so now.

5. Handling lots of responsibilities is actually enjoyable, providing you do just that: you learn to handle them. It's also the mark of being a fully fledged adult. There aren't many of us. We're the few, the proud, the burdened. But we soldier on, and that's the key.

Let them taunt you, push you around a little, and even get in your face. Just keep making progress, and all of these obstacles will fall away, and you'll still be standing, with a grin on your face and with more energy than ever!

Chapter Six

Script Your Success

Read my articles and books and get to know me even a little, and you'll learn I'm a systems person, on top of being fairly intuitive.

I admire individuals and businesses that figure out how to deliver value across time and space and cultures, especially the ones that build enterprises in traditional service fields.

McDonald's is one such business. It has done a spectacular job of providing substantially the same burgers and cleanliness and friendly customer service across more than half a century and around the globe. When I worked for an experimental division of that company, named after founder Ray Kroc, I learned how to do things the McDonald's way, which is a discipline as much as it is a skill.

So when I went on to become a collector, a salesperson, and a manager of and consultant for these functions along with customer service, I saw the merit in using

SCRIPTS: patterned talks that are almost as predictable as the way you're supposed to make a hamburger or clean a countertop. Scripts are explicit conversational guides that pave the way to success.

Why leave the cooking of a meal to chance when you can plan and control its quality nearly every time? Ditto for conversations. If your intention is to communicate clearly, to sell, or to perform a service, why permit outcomes to be random affairs when you can hit the mark, informing, selling, and satisfying with uncanny accuracy?

At this point in my career, I am responsible for crafting call paths that have been employed nearly as many times as McDonald's has sold burgers. I suppose that's why I'm particularly concerned when scripts fail, when they sound dumb. As an example, let's take the supermarket where I do much of my shopping. When handing me my bags, the clerk asks, "Would you like help out to your car?"

It's a nice gesture, and potentially a perfect customer-service message. It says: "I'm ready, willing, and able to help."

That's always nice to hear, and as a general rule it adds goodie points to the store's service account in the customer's mind. It builds goodwill. (Once I asked a checker how many times out of 100 customers actually accept the offered help. "Only once or twice," she said.)

I'm a big guy with an athlete's ego, and when I hear this otherwise sweet and kind offer, I think: "What am I, falling apart?"

This comes to mind when I've bought only a half-gallon of milk or a six-pack of soda. If I need assistance to carry those, I'm in big trouble and have to start hitting the weights and the exercise bike.

In other words, the gesture fails and actually back-fires when there is little to carry and the person seems physically fit. It sounds absurd.

Scripts are useful, but when you need to *not* use one, to depart from the planned patter, have the good sense to do so in time.

Same supermarket, but this time let's look at script 2. At the bottom of each receipt it says, YOU SAVED whatever the amount is by logging in your club member-ship number. The clerk reads this aloud just before he or she hands the receipt to me.

But one time, the person was so much on autopilot with her script that she failed to read ahead before announcing: "And today, Mr. Goodman, you saved, uh, NOTHING!"

That's right. Every single item in my cart was full price, so the script absolutely failed. And in a way it impeached the credibility of the entire "savings" banter. If I saved nothing, well, "Thanks for nothing" is what I ended up chortling to myself.

This reminds me of the other night when I phoned my website hosting service.

One tool I share in my customer-service teachings is the transition phrase. Typically, it consists of a concilia-tory set of words, followed by vital information. If you want to send a crystal clear relationship message, one of these can help.

"Well, I understand that" is an often-heard transition phrase. Used in a timely and appropriate way:

1. It builds an emotional bridge to the client, as if we're saying, "I get you" or "I know where you're coming from" or "I can relate."

2. It says, "You don't have to continue explaining. I see the problem."

3. And it tacitly says, "We're in the same boat; you're not abnormal to say what you have said."

That's pretty cool stuff, and quite impressive when you consider that a little phrase can clearly conjure up so much so fast. But there is a dark side to this technique, when it seems absolutely insincere. Consequently it fails as a device, potentially ruining not only a conversation but also a customer relationship.

The other night, when I called in for help in adjusting an erroneous billing statement issued by my web host, the customer service rep said: "I understand that" and then, defying all logic, steadfastly refused to apply proper credit to my account.

I blasted back, "You *don't* understand, because if you did appreciate the error, and you calculated the credit properly, you'd make the precise adjustment I've asked for!"

"Well, I understand," she replied once more, absolutely on autopilot at this point, crashing the conversation.

May I make a clear point to her and to everyone else? *Understanding necessitates action.* If you are a parent and you understand that your infant is crying because she has wet her diaper, you change it right away. You eliminate the offensive condition.

Coddling the little creampuff with cooing and cajoling won't work. If there is a physical cause, you invoke a physical cure, and pronto!

I hope to sell you on the value of using smart scripts, ones that are adjustable to various audiences and occasions as well as to different media. But it's important to note that being sold on their use doesn't mean others will adopt them with open arms. You might agree with me that scripts are to conversations what systems are to franchisers such as McDonald's, but this doesn't mean you'll avoid resistance if you try to get others to agree.

Why won't your sales, customer-service, technical-support, and professional associates willingly use scripts? Given any wiggle room, most people will slip out of implementing these meant-to-be-helpful tools.

Is resistance of this sort rational or irrational? Are these folks enabling or disabling themselves through script avoidance?

As a veteran practitioner and consultant in business-to-business and business-to-consumer sales, service, and technical support, I've seen people go to great lengths to escape scripting, even at the expense of losing their jobs.

Managers have cajoled, threatened, and rewarded to encourage script use, with much the same outcome. They walk through their service centers and sales bull pens and hear a different speech being uttered by every voice in the room.

Instead of conducting a symphony, where everyone knows the score and is literally on the same page, leaders and trainers hear continuing cacophony, conversational chaos. What's up with this?

Is it worth your effort to introduce, polish, and police a master script that all are expected to use?

The answer to this question is a solid, unequivocal *maybe*. You need to be willing to be more thorough than you have ever been in introducing and sustaining scripts if you expect compliance and a big payoff from their use.

Scripts can and should work, but they have little chance of proving their value until people use them. But if they won't even try them out, what evidence do you have to support your contention that scripts will do better than an unscripted approach?

If you want your people to use scripts, you'll need to hail a CAB.

There are three challenges facing managers: (1) cognitive, (2) affective, and (3) behavioral. We must change what our reps KNOW about scripts, how they FEEL about them, and most importantly, how they BEHAVE with regard to them.

Most people try to skip steps 1 and 2 and jump to step 3.

They say, "Just try it! You'll see. It will work!" Then they're amazed that reps won't budge.

By enhancing what reps know about scripts, we move people along a continuum from ignorance to enlightenment. People need to know a few vital things about scripts.

Optimally, these pointers are delivered in seminars and small group briefings.

For one thing, scripts are inevitable. You cannot escape using one. Why?

Language is redundant: it repeats itself. (See?) Moreover, as survival-seeking beings, our brains are hard-wired to notice patterns that succeed, whether it's stalking the weakest caribou in the herd or pouncing on prospects that say, "Yes, we have a budget for what you're selling!"

Precursors to success repeat themselves in our presentations. If we sneeze during a crucial part of the talk and a prospect suddenly loosens up and becomes more agreeable, we'll sneeze or cough unconsciously. Later we'll even purposely inject a pratfall as our talks arrive at roughly the same point.

Scriptmasters notice these critical coincidences and exploit them. They're able to listen to chats that succeed and fail and to glean from them the dos and don'ts that are generally inaudible to the rest of us.

They make what is mostly tacit, explicit. There is a hidden design to success, they believe, that eludes novices and others that insist on winging their calls.

Scriptmasters and wise managers also appreciate that the shortest call path to a sale or to a pleased client is a straight line, and extemporized talks are often unnecessarily circuitous and long-winded. In short, scripts promise efficiency and effectiveness. You'll sell more, service better, and provide even a higher quality of tech support when you use a script. And you'll save time.

But let's say all of these things are true, and your reps now *know* why scripts work, that they are inevitable, that they will exist whether they are written down or seem to pop out of our mouths; what then? Will they use them, now that they know more?

No.

Knowing and doing are two different challenges. Bridging them is the matter of how we *feel* about scripts, the *affective* dimension of our attitudes. By adjusting how people feel about using scripts, we move them along a continuum from a negative to a positive attitude and from outright resistance to tentative acceptance.

We need to work this feeling part of the equation from a few different angles.

First, we need to appreciate that many people feel that using a script makes them at best low-level workers. They think scripts create a spirit-sapping assembly line in a conversation factory, transforming them into mere robots. Did they graduate from high school and start or finish college and obtain professional certifications for *this*? To be whipped into compliance? To be cogs in the machine, or worse, the machine itself?

Many people feel scripts are phony, are inherently untruthful and manipulative.

You'll hear them lament, "I'm not an actor!" and "I want to be *me*!" These are immature, adolescent, and naïve reactions, but they're real.

Associates and colleagues don't quite get the fact that they'll be role-playing for their entire lives, as long as they need others for sustenance, love, assistance of any kind.

Moreover, they'll need to squelch that insistent "me, me, me" brat voice to get along with others simply and effectively wherever they are.

And we, like surrogate parents or big brothers and sisters, have to break this real-world news to them.

Some job candidates have likened scripts to serving fast food, and have snickered, "I don't want to work at McDonald's!"

I love this, because it gives me a chance to lecture them on the genius of Ray Kroc and the human systems he created for assuring cleanliness and delivering successful food service worldwide, irrespective of diverse languages, cultures, and suppliers, and even in the face of antagonistic political and economic systems.

I get to tell them how I worked for an experimental unit of McDonald's called Raymond's, in the middle of Beverly Hills, across the street from Tiffany and Company.

Kroc built a true jewel of a company based on scripting nearly everything humans do at work.

I was cleaning my own kitchen counter the other day, and a smile crossed my lips after I asked myself the question, "Why am I so finicky about cleaning up before and after meals?"

"Because you were trained to do it!" a voice bellowed from inside of me. Guess who trained me? The same folks Ray Kroc trained.

Once we start to respect scripts as tools for financial success and even for life success, we start to attack the second challenge of making them work, and making our people work them.

We drill down to core emotional resistance. Scripts aren't barnacles that prevent ships from sailing smoothly. Scripts are the engines, the sails, the captain and crew, and the laws of the sea, all rolled into one.

The final part of the scripting vehicle, the CAB, is *behavioral.* Your people can know more and feel less negatively about using scripts, but they are paid to put them to work. I've found the best way to get people to use and to keep using a master script is to offer this open challenge: "If you can write and stick to a better script, show it to me. If I think it has a chance, I'll let you test it, after we have established a baseline for using the master script. If yours beats the master, you get to keep using it until your performance falls below room average. Who knows? If yours is effective enough, maybe it will become the new master, and there may even be a bonus in it for you!"

What does this say? Scripts are here to stay. If you don't like ours, beat it with yours in a controlled experiment. We don't care what system works, providing it is honest and you work the system. What we do know is that improvisation, winging it, and being unsystematic are pathways to failure.

The worst script, in other words, is trying to have no script at all.

Every point of resistance I have just attributed to using scripts is probably a sore point with you as well. But if you want to succeed time and again in creating crystal clear communications, why reinvent the wheel with every conversation? Identify what works for you, and for your associates if you are responsible for other people, and then stick to it. As the old adage says, plan your work and then work your plan.

Be on your game when an encounter calls for a customized response instead of a memorized one, and use what is appropriate to the occasion.

Bringing Scripts to Life

Scripts work much of the time, and when we're lucky, most of the time. But they never work all of the time.

When I write scripts for customer service and for selling, I test them, tweak them here and there, and then I deploy them at my clients' sites.

Minimally, it's a systematic process of validation, and once my scripts have been proven in dozens, hundreds, thousands and even millions of conversations, I can say, very authoritatively, that they work.

From my standpoint it is important to be as scientific as possible, not only to be dispensing solutions that are assured of producing sales and customer satisfaction, but to overcome the perennial cynicism that salespeople, customer-service reps, and their managers bring to scripts. There is always the question, "Will this work?" But an even more pertinent one is, "Will it work for me?"

The answer is always the same: unless you're an alien from a distant galaxy, of course it will work for you.

But this isn't the whole story, as you might imagine. As a trainer, manager, and consultant, I've seen that scripts are only part of the answer. They're helpful and even necessary ingredients of success, but we need more to succeed. Specifically, we need direction in bringing them to life.

This is where mere vendors of scripts miss the mark. They might advertise a script for getting insurance appointments, but without the appropriate instructions for breathing vitality into them, it's like showing words on a page to an eight-month-old: they're gibberish.

Let me give you a quick example of a way of getting through call screening that I invented that should double the frequency with which you succeed.

Instead of asking, "Is Bill Smith in?" which launches secretarial countermeasures, starting with the universal "May I tell him who's calling?" we shift the dynamics entirely.

"Hello, Gary Goodman, Customersatisfaction.com, for Bill Smith please, thank you."

I invite you to reverse-engineer this winning gambit at your leisure, and you'll see many fascinating, nontraditional facets to it. But for now, let me point out that a script needs three T's to succeed, as I have mentioned in a previous chapter.

It needs the proper *text*, *tone*, and *timing*.

Let's just look at how one of the T's—timing—affects the delivery of the screening line I provided.

Purposely, I don't pause before uttering the words "Thank you," because I want those words to be *final* for the screener to fetch the person I'm requesting. If I pause before saying, "Thank you," the screener will interpret this as a relinquishing of the call to her and will encourage her to ask another disqualifying question. (You're unlikely to figure this out on your own, because we normally pause at punctuation instead of talking through it.)

My first-generation trainees, the ones whose companies bring me in to speak, to consult, and to write scripts, receive this instruction, but their imitators don't. That's why those I haven't directed sound canned and their scripts "aren't working," or so they claim.

To be accurate, they should say, the scripts aren't working *for them*.

Again, scripts are essential to success in all walks of life, especially for selling yourself and your ideas and providing top customer service, but they need to be accompanied by the proper direction and training.

Let's put what you have learned to work, shall we? Specifically, I think it would be of major benefit for you to take some time now to script some of the most challenging communication situations YOU face.

I wrote a book a few years back called *Please Don't Shoot the Messenger! How to Talk to Demanding Bosses, Clueless Colleagues, Tough Customers, and Difficult Clients without Losing Your Cool (Or Your Job!)*

You can kick off from the subtitle, if you wish, for your inspiration.

Do you have a demanding boss? Need a little less stress or to renegotiate work rules? Maybe it's time to spend a little quality time with him or her and discuss matters.

Quick, how about a PEP talk?

What's your POINT?

"I could use a raise."

What's your EVIDENCE?

"Since we've downsized, I've been doing two jobs. I'm investing up to sixty hours per week. And I'd love some recognition."

"So I could use a raise."

Back to your POINT, right?

What did I leave out, if I want to be persuasive? That's right, I didn't tie it down with an OK, did I?

"So, I could use a raise, OK?"

That's better.

What clear communications do you need to send at work? Take this time to identify three circumstances in which you need a better script.

Now write a rough draft of each one.

Likewise, note three situations in your personal life in which you need to communicate with crystal clarity. Write these down, and compose rough drafts.

Now take a look at what you have in front of you.

Is everything crystal clear? Probably not, at least not yet, so let's troubleshoot some improvements, shall we?

Is your text too long or too short? If it's too long, is that a result of redundancies? Are you needlessly saying the same thing twice or more, without good cause?

Cross out the needless verbiage. Does that help?

Is your text confusing? Does it seem aimless?

Have you told them where you're going, did you go there, and have you recapped where you have been?

Maybe you have buried the lead—making your most important point midway through your talk or script.

Your listeners or readers may have tuned out by the time you reach your point.

If it's major, if it's what you aim to get across first and foremost, why not make it first and foremost?

In other words, make it your headline.

Is your tone friendly or unfriendly? One tip-off is the number of "I" words you use instead of "you" or "we" words. Do you sound like a raging egotist, making one self-centered proclamation after the next? Or does your chat involve mutuality, equality, a feeling that we're in this thing together?

Prune your scripts for any possibility that they will seem unfriendly.

For example, I was just about to finish an email that started with the words "Still no check."

I have been waiting for the better part of a week to receive one by mail, yet here we are: with just a few weeks to go before doing an international conference, I have booked and paid for my flight, so I'm out of pocket, and I haven't received the down payment on my speaking fee.

After the "Still no check" overture, I went on to ask to what address had it been sent and through which carrier if not the mail service.

But I did what I have been suggesting you do here. I did a friendliness check and found my email sorely lacking in the sweet milk of human kindness.

In the middle of the last paragraph I stopped abruptly and walked down the street to check the mail. There it was—the long-awaited check, as promised.

I was thrilled that I took the extra few seconds to pause before hitting the SEND button.

Now that you have crafted your most important scripts, it's time to test them. This is the fun part, because you get to assess their clout, to determine how well they are working.

Crystal-Clarity Action Plan

I write nearly every day. In fact, I was just honored with a "100 Articles in 100 Days" award from Ezinearticles .com, where I post many of my pieces. I start with this fact for two reasons:

First, I think it's always important to know the credentials of your presenter, and especially that he practices what he preaches; and second, that a commitment to daily improvement must be a major part of your thirty-day action plan.

Why every day? We need to create new habits. Some say a new habit needs six or twelve weeks to start becoming automatic. I suspect the actual number of days, weeks, or months is really highly individualized. For example, decades ago, I stopped smoking, and I am grateful that I did. But even a few years after the physical manifestations were gone, the cravings and actual use of tobacco, I would have dreams at night during which I lit up. Amazing, how some old habits, and I suppose in this case addictions, hold sway over us.

So our thirty-day action plan is really about the *first* thirty days. Personally, I believe striving for crystal clarity in our communications is a lifetime pursuit, but the best way to get under way is by undoing our negative inertia while putting into place purposeful, positive practices.

Let me share with you a story that demonstrates how practice is the key to better speaking and writing. One of the best communication classes I ever took in college was with an instructor who had a good academic background from Stanford, but more importantly, he was one of Dale Carnegie's initial cohort of trainers.

A member and past president of Toastmasters International, Sheldon Hayden loved to speak, and I'm sure he was most gratified by the adoration he received from pleased-as-punch audiences. One secret to his success as a speech teacher was the fact that at each class, every student had to deliver at least one brief talk. Add those one-minute chats to the formal speeches that we also had to deliver, and this meant during a semester we would be giving somewhere around twenty-five speeches.

That is a lot of experience "popping off on your hind feet," as he used to colloquially call it. With all of those successes under one's belt, how could a student *not* improve?

Frankly, that was impossible. Failure wasn't an option, because if you speak enough, you'll become competent. Speak more, and you'll grow adept. Outdo that level of performance, and you'll excel, and probably learn to enjoy it immensely, as I did.

I have come to embrace and apply this principle, also known as the law of large numbers, to nearly every endeavor. If you're a salesperson, make more contacts, and they'll turn into more prospects, and these will turn into more sales.

If you are a writer, do a lot of it, more than you ever thought you could. Sooner or later, you'll feel capable of writing anything anytime. See my book and audio program, *The Law of Large Numbers: How to Make Success Inevitable*.

Someone once defined *luck* as preparation meeting opportunity.

I look at it this way: prepare a lot, and you'll meet even more opportunities than you ever imagined, creating your own luck along the way.

Watching Mr. Hayden leave our class and hop into his silver-blue Cadillac convertible with white-leather interior, his navy blazer set off by his shock of white hair, always gave me the impression he was very lucky indeed, as were those of us that studied with him and emulated his example.

Do you need training in public speaking?

As I mentioned earlier, Stanford researchers found 80 percent of Americans are shy in at least some situations. Let me give this a different emphasis here as we undertake action. Eighty percent of us are *situationally shy*. This means we are shy at some times and in some places, but not necessarily in all. It is crucial to emphasize this fact.

You might be petrified to give a speech at a convention or a business conference, and you could very well be in the habit of turning down one opportunity after another.

However, you might be a stunner in job interviews, top-drawer, coming across as a really calm and poised professional.

If you're a manager, you could loathe one-to-one performance appraisals, gazing into an associate's eyeballs and clearly saying, "Sorry, but this level of performance isn't cutting it!" Yet standing before a work unit, you could feel quite comfortable sharing the bad news that unless productivity is enhanced, there could be some work furloughs.

When I was in junior high, I was tapped to star in the musical *The Emperor's New Clothes*. This role required acting and singing. While I do not remember many details of the performance, apart from having to kiss the highly powdered cheek of the female lead, I suppose I did fairly well.

I went on to enjoy drama classes in high school and to leads in other, more serious plays. But public speaking, for me, was an acquired taste. I've tried to analyze why I drew a line between being on stage as an actor and being on stage as an orator. After all, there are lots of similarities. For one thing, there is an audience. You are performing. If you do well, they tend to applaud you at the end. (Even if you don't, polite people will still applaud.)

But stagecraft and speechcraft differ in material ways. First, on stage your lines have already been prepared for you. Second, unless you're starring in a one-person show, there are others that are helping to carry the performance. Third, plays are entertainment; they are to be enjoyed.

When public speaking, it's all about you, baby. You rise or fall on your own, and on the strength of your language choices and delivery characteristics. And when you're delivering an address, typically there is something important at stake. You aren't present to entertain, unless you are a professional that has been retained to roast a celebrity or produce gales of laughter. You're probably in front of folks to make a serious point, to elicit their support for a cause or a company. And ultimately the power of your ideas and how you marshal and express them is what informs how your audience will react.

It's fair to say that there are vital differences between speech and drama, and between interpersonal, one-to-one, small-group or work-team occasions and public speaking.

Still, if you do more, and you work the law of large numbers, you'll polish your act in any circumstance. I know professional TV and film actors who gladly take on roles in local or regional community-theater companies. They do this because work begets work. They gain exposure and have showcases to which they can invite their industry contacts and agents. Above all, they keep their performance tools sharpened. Actors learn and improve by acting, and speakers, by speaking.

Once I was doing a seminar in Braintree, Massachusetts. About forty people signed up. It was a beautiful autumn day, leaves falling in their spectacular New England hues. Only one problem: my voice was fading away with each passing second because of laryngitis.

By the time the program began, I had little more than a stage whisper that I could summon. Fearing that I'd be down to using pantomime and chicken scratches on my flip chart by program's end, I recalled a lesson that I learned from my high-school drama teacher, John Ingle: "Stay disciplined, and no matter what happens, the show must go on!"

As it turned out, my course evaluations were very high, and not one person criticized my flagging voice.

I attribute my fading voice partly to the sheer number of seminars I was doing at the time. But my professional response to difficulty also sprang from the sheer number of seminars I was doing. Because I was used to the rigors of travel and the physical demands of putting out robust energy day after day, I carried on and came up a winner.

Where can you get speaking experience? We improve by doing, by performing, so take and make more opportunities to express yourself. Toastmasters is an organization that will get you up on your feet meeting after meeting. If you attend their sessions, you'll be treated to a very positive atmosphere in which to develop your skills.

You can sign up for a fundamentals of public speaking class at a junior college, and I highly recommend it. First, it will teach you how to organize various kinds of presentations geared to informing, persuading, and inspiring. Second, you'll learn how to organize your ideas, echoing and building upon the information you learned here.

And third, you'll sharpen your delivery skills while diminishing your stage fright.

By the way—and this is something most people don't realize—you can usually take classes on a pass/no pass or noncredit basis. This relieves the pressure on you to perform at any pace that is imposed by others or that invokes external standards of excellence. As far as I am concerned, simply signing up for a class is a huge victory in itself.

You should also know that there is nothing to prevent you from repeating a class, not because you think you have failed or to improve a grade, but for personal enhancement. You might even want to sign up for the same class but with a different instructor each time.

Some colleges have a neatly laid out series of performance-based classes. For example, in a typical communications curriculum you can expect to find a class in fundamentals of public speaking, as I mentioned earlier. There might be an intermediate or advanced public-speaking class as well. I took both, and while the bar was set a little higher in the second course, it wasn't very much. It was certainly within reach. A communications curriculum may also have classes in interpersonal communication, nonverbal communication, group communication, and business communication. So you can invest months and years in continuously improving your speaking skills, while also enjoying the typically modest course fees that community colleges charge.

I also suggest you consider joining a community chapter of a well-known service organization, such as the

Optimists, Lions, and Rotary International. You'll get many chances to serve and chair committees and make presentations before local and regional meetings.

I've been a guest speaker on many occasions at service organizations, and I can tell you that they are filled with intelligent, positive people, and they make marvelously receptive audiences.

Your Fears Will Change to Cheers!

You may have figured this out for yourself, but I should explicitly say that the distinction in my comfort levels before dramatic audiences and public-speaking audiences disappeared over time. So much so that I became a professional public speaker. Part of my success is attributable to the wisdom that was shared with me about what I could expect as a speaker, which I shared at the beginning of this book: *you'll never seem as nervous on the outside as you feel on the inside*. When we're waiting to be introduced or we're going to do the honors ourselves, it's easy to overreact to our bodily signals. Our hands may feel cold and clammy, we could be perspiring, and we could also feel a shortness of breath. Don't worry: the audience cannot feel what you're feeling.

We can do one of two things with these signals: (1) we can monitor them and start telling ourselves we're losing control and soon we'll be an utter, complete mess, or (2) we can interpret these signals as excitement, as exhilaration. Novices do the former, and professionals do the latter, and that makes all the difference. We learn to enjoy public speaking, and some of us build our careers on it, even if we started out being very shy.

Remember These Three Points

1. Through systematic desensitization, you can overcome most if not all of your fears and concerns about communication.
2. By using your imagination constructively, you will envision positive results, and your unconscious will assist you in bringing about the visions you have postulated.
3. Prayer helps!

The law of large numbers involves the first principle mentioned above: systematically desensitizing yourself to your fears. For instance, someone afraid of cats might start overcoming this problem by watching kittens at play. Then she might talk to cats, meowing and cooing, while hearing the little beings communicating back. Finally, she might softly pet a kitty and hold it in her hands.

Inch by inch, it's a cinch: this is the prescription for using systematic desensitization, whether you want to overcome a fear of riding elevators or conquering stage fright. Gradual improvements precede more ambitious ones.

Systematic conditioning is powerful because it is behavioral. It makes us do things differently, moving us from the sidelines to the center of the action. But we should also work the other two elements of the equation: the mental and spiritual dimensions of improvement.

We improve first in the mind. One of my earliest public-speaking teachers, Mrs. Gibbons in high school, used a visualization exercise. She started with an image of us feeling sweaty and nervous, our voices squeaking and quaking and our knees knocking as we walked to the podium. Naturally everyone disliked that experience.

Next, she had us erase that image and substitute a different one. I'll take you through it now:

Imagine feeling a tingling sensation in your head, a little bit of a chill, a rush of excitement, as if you are going to play a sport and hit a ball or jump out of the blocks in a footrace. The time has come to shine, to stand out, to distinguish yourself, to WIN! That same feeling of impending triumph, the sense that there is a sweet smell of success in the air, a feeling of joyous, positive anticipation, is starting to fill your with a warm glow. This is YOUR day, your time to shine, and you are starting to glow already.

You look back on your preparation with great appreciation and pride. You have paid the price of success. You know your topic better than anyone else in your class. You are the expert, and everyone respects and knows it. In fact, your audience is looking forward to seeing and hearing your succeed, wildly, beyond your fondest dreams. Watch them clapping their hands, hear those cheers as you conclude your talk. You have earned them, and each time to speak you are getting better and better. You are enjoying every second of it!

Now take one deep breath!

Breath Control

Most of us pay far too little attention to our breathing. But breathing properly is essential to succeeding as a speaker.

Let me tell you who does pay sufficient attention, because certain professionals depend on optimized breathing. Among others:

1. Singers need breath control to interpret music appropriately.
2. Actors need breath control, especially if they want to be heard in the back seats of theaters.
3. Martial artists need it so they won't exhaust their air supply before a battle is over.

I studied Chinese Kenpo Karate for eight rigorous years at a dojo, and one of the most important lessons was to optimize our breathing. This means we cannot afford to run out of breath, to exhaust ourselves, to fall into an oxygen debt. Yet novice speakers suffer exactly from this condition. They let their nerves get the better of them and they hyperventilate, taking a succession of shallow breaths instead of deeper, longer ones. By the time they reach the podium or platform, they sound like they have just done a 100-yard dash—nearly breathless.

This oxygen debt makes them sound nervous, first to themselves, which induces them to panic breathing, which is even shorter and shallower. By this time, the audience is feeling insecure for the speaker, worrying that she is going to lose control, and their faces appear concerned and furrowed. The speaker monitors their distraction and feels even more insecure, exacerbating a sense of panic. By this time, she is lucky to simply survive the ordeal.

How do we avoid this scenario?

BY BREATHING SLOWLY AND DEEPLY IN ADVANCE!

Specifically, at least two minutes before you are going to perform, take at least one deep breath, exhaling slowly. Then do some normal breathing and repeat the deep, slow breath.

This will do many positive things. First, it will calm you down considerably. Second, it will send oxygen to your brain and muscles, helping you to think clearly and perform at your best physically. Additionally, by having more air in your lungs, you'll deepen your voice.

Deepening your voice: why is this important?

A deeper voice, by its very nature, doesn't sound stressed or squeaky. It is the controlled tone with which we should begin most orations, because we want our talks to reach a crescendo, to peak at the end, we have to have room to move up tonally. If we start at the highest point in our vocal range, we're stuck and have nowhere to go except down, which is anticlimactic and disappointing.

By the way, when we have more breath, we can speak at a slower pace, which also lends (forgive me) an air of authority to our performances.

So remember to breathe in advance, and continue to take deep breaths between your points so you can have at your command the rich vocal range you are naturally endowed with.

One more thing: when your tones sound mellow and not rushed, you'll hear it for yourself, which will give you positive feedback during your speech. Noticing you're in control, you'll be pleased with yourself, which will contribute to your ease and relaxation during the remainder of your talk.

The Message You're Fixing Is You!

Quintilian, an ancient Roman orator of note, defined eloquence as "the good man speaking well." His emphasis on the character, the ethos, the credibility of the speaker was paramount. If your motives are good and you have a noble purpose, the means will come to you for expressing them properly and well.

But speaking and writing clearly aren't only matters of character, important as that may be. As you've learned from this book, there are many techniques that need to be summoned as well to promote easy and quick understanding and to persuade.

I think good speaking and effective writing build on themselves. If you practice the law of large numbers, seizing every chance you can get to express yourself, you'll improve, and clarity will become a beacon and a destination. Through repeated acts of clear expression, you'll refine your thinking. Your own motives will become clearer to you. And your standards will increase with your increased challenges and your proper responses to them.

Psychologist William James, in a different context, described how feelings, attitudes, and behaviors reinforce each other. He asked: "Do we run because we're afraid, or are we afraid because we run?"

The answer is both. Generally, seeing a snake or a predator will make us run. But in the course of running we also breathe quickly, our pulses and heartbeats race, and adrenalin courses through our veins. Monitoring these signs of fear, we feel the emotion of fear. One thing feeds on another.

The same phenomenon applies to writing and speaking clearly. We are clear because we write and speak, and we write and speak because we are clear about what we want to accomplish and the means with which to do it.

While appealing to our audiences is one of our main aims in endeavoring to communicate clearly, by no means is it the most important.

I would argue that with each speech we utter and with every note we compose, we are improving ourselves, and this is one glorious purpose that can be never-ending.

Robert Pirsig's *Zen and the Art of Motorcycle Maintenance* is a fictional narrative of a cross-country motorcycle trip taken by a character and his son. The protagonist is a professor of rhetoric in Montana, where our journey begins.

He asks his English composition students a deceptively simple question, something similar to what I have been implicitly asking throughout this book:

"What is quality?"

Pirsig's character delves into the quality question so deeply that it vexes his students and himself. It's a great read, and I recommend it to you, if only for one of his conclusions, which is pertinent to us now that we are about to say, "Happy trails."

Pirsig discovers that the motorcycle that we're working on is really *ourselves*.

When you approach communications with a quality frame of mind, you're relaxed and patient, and above all self-accepting.

If you approach your task properly, you can fix anything, and I'm sure you will.

Please tell me how this book has helped you, and let's stay in touch! I do personal and corporate coaching, training, and keynote speaking. I can be reached here:

Dr. Gary S. Goodman

(818) 970-GARY (4279)

drgaryscottgoodman@yahoo.com

gary@drgarygoodman.com

gary@customersatisfaction.com

gary@negotiationschool.com

Good luck!

Printed in the USA
CPSIA information can be obtained
at www.ICGtesting.com
JSHW012035140824
68134JS00033B/3080